A JOHN CATT PUBLICATION

C000089609

Knowledge Quiz

Religious Studies

Christianity

Dawn Cox

With thanks to Louise Hutton and Ruth Jackson

First published 2020

by John Catt Educational Ltd,
15 Riduna Park, Station Road,
Melton, Woodbridge IP12 1QT

Tel: +44 (0) 1394 389850
Email: enquiries@johncatt.com
Website: www.johncatt.com

ISBN: 978 1 912906 77 2

Set and designed by John Catt Educational Ltd

1	Start with Quiz 1. Use the answer key to memorise the facts and quotations.
2	If you see anything unfamiliar, make sure you look it up or ask your teacher about it.
3	When you're ready, complete the first quiz from memory.
4	Mark it using the answer key.
5	Record your score in the quiz tracker.
6	Leave it a few days, then try the same quiz again. We've rearranged the order of the questions on the quiz sheets to further challenge your knowledge retrieval.
7	Keep completing the same quiz every few days until you get full marks every time.
8	Move on to the next quiz and repeat steps 1–8.
9	Revisit previously mastered quizzes after a few weeks or months to check you still know the content.

Which quizzes should I complete?

This book is for users of all exam boards. Most of the quizzes cover core knowledge that is part of all specifications. Some quizzes are marked **Core+** – these contain questions that may go beyond the knowledge needed in your specification, or may appear only in some specifications (check your exam board specification to find out).

Important!

This book will help you memorise most of the knowledge needed for the Christianity exam in your Religious Studies GCSE. Some question content is repeated to help you learn it. There are many other things you need to do to prepare for your exams – including lots and lots of practice. Memorising facts and quotations gives you the fundamental knowledge you need, and being able to **apply** that knowledge is the next challenge.

Contents

Beliefs and teachings

ANSWER KEY

1.1	What does 'omnipotent' mean when describing the nature of God?	God is all-powerful
1.2	What does 'omniscient' mean when describing the nature of God?	God is all-knowing/seeing
1.3	What does 'omnibenevolent' mean when describing the nature of God?	God is all-good/loving
1.4	What does 'just' mean when describing the nature of God?	God is fair and will treat us fairly at judgement
1.5	What does 'omnipresent' mean when describing the nature of God?	God is present everywhere
1.6	What does 'judge' mean when describing the nature of God?	At judgement, God will judge all humans on their actions in this life
1.7	What does 'eternal' mean when describing the nature of God?	God has no beginning and no end. He will exist forever
1.8	What does 'transcendent' mean when describing the nature of God?	God is beyond and outside of creation
1.9	What does 'forgiving' mean when describing the nature of God?	God will forgive humans of their sins
1.10	What does 'immanent' mean when describing the nature of God?	God is within and involved with creation

What does 'immanent' mean when describing the nature of God?	
What does 'omnipotent' mean when describing the nature of God?	
What does 'omnipresent' mean when describing the nature of God?	
What does 'judge' mean when describing the nature of God?	
What does 'omniscient' mean when describing the nature of God?	
What does 'forgiving' mean when describing the nature of God?	
What does 'eternal' mean when describing the nature of God?	
What does 'transcendent' mean when describing the nature of God?	
What does 'omnibenevolent' mean when describing the nature of God?	
What does 'just' mean when describing the nature of God?	

Quiz 2: The nature of God 2

ANSWER KEY

2.1	'Our _ _ _ _ _ _ in heaven' (Matthew 6:9–15/Lord's Prayer)	Father
2.2	'If you _ _ _ _ _ _ _ other people when they sin against you, your heavenly Father will also _ _ _ _ _ _ _ you' (Matthew 6:9–15)	forgive
2.3	'For God so loved the world that he gave his one and only _ _ _' (John 3:16)	son
2.4	'God created _ _ _ _ _ _ _ _ _ _ _ _, making them to be like himself. He created them male and female' (Genesis 1:27)	human beings
2.5	What is the meaning of 'incarnation' in Christianity?	God became flesh – his son Jesus Christ was born
2.6	What aspect of God is described in Genesis 1:1–30?	God as (omnipotent) creator
2.7	How many 'persons' are there in the Trinity?	Three
2.8	'You shall have no other _ _ _ _ before me' (Ten Commandments, Exodus 20)	gods
2.9	'I, the Lord your God, am a _ _ _ _ _ _ _ God' (Ten Commandments, Exodus 20)	jealous
2.10	'We believe in _ _ _ God' (Nicene Creed)	one

TRACKER

Quiz	Date	Score
1		
2		
3		
4		
5		
6		

Got it? ☐

Quiz 2: The nature of God 2

2.1	'Our _ _ _ _ _ _ in heaven' (Matthew 6:9–15/Lord's Prayer)	
2.2	'If you _ _ _ _ _ _ _ other people when they sin against you, your heavenly Father will also _ _ _ _ _ _ _ you' (Matthew 6:9–15)	
2.3	'For God so loved the world that he gave his one and only _ _ _' (John 3:16)	
2.4	'God created _ _ _ _ _ _ _ _ _ _ _, making them to be like himself. He created them male and female' (Genesis 1:27)	
2.5	What is the meaning of 'incarnation' in Christianity?	
2.6	What aspect of God is described in Genesis 1:1–30?	
2.7	How many 'persons' are there in the Trinity?	
2.8	'You shall have no other _ _ _ _ _ _ before me' (Ten Commandments, Exodus 20)	
2.9	'I, the Lord your God, am a _ _ _ _ _ _ _ God' (Ten Commandments, Exodus 20)	
2.10	'We believe in _ _ _ God' (Nicene Creed)	

'For God so loved the world that he gave his one and only ___' (John 3:16)	
What aspect of God is described in Genesis 1:1–30?	
'I, the Lord your God, am a _____ God' (Ten Commandments, Exodus 20)	
'If you _____ other people when they sin against you, your heavenly Father will also _____ you' (Matthew 6:9–15)	
'God created _____ _____, making them to be like himself. He created them male and female' (Genesis 1:27)	
'You shall have no other ____ before me' (Ten Commandments, Exodus 20)	
'We believe in ___ God' (Nicene Creed)	
'Our _____ in heaven' (Matthew 6:9–15/Lord's Prayer)	
What is the meaning of 'incarnation' in Christianity?	
How many 'persons' are there in the Trinity?	

'We believe in _ _ _ God' (Nicene Creed)	
'Our _ _ _ _ _ _ in heaven' (Matthew 6:9–15/Lord's Prayer)	
What is the meaning of 'incarnation' in Christianity?	
What aspect of God is described in Genesis 1:1–30?	
'If you _ _ _ _ _ _ _ other people when they sin against you, your heavenly Father will also _ _ _ _ _ _ _ you' (Matthew 6:9–15)	
'I, the Lord your God, am a _ _ _ _ _ _ _ God' (Ten Commandments, Exodus 20)	
How many 'persons' are there in the Trinity?	
'You shall have no other _ _ _ _ before me' (Ten Commandments, Exodus 20)	
'For God so loved the world that he gave his one and only _ _ _' (John 3:16)	
'God created _ _ _ _ _ _ _ _ _ _ _, making them to be like himself. He created them male and female' (Genesis 1:27)	

'We believe in _ _ _ God' (Nicene Creed)	
'Our _ _ _ _ _ _ in heaven' (Matthew 6:9–15/Lord's Prayer)	
What is the meaning of 'incarnation' in Christianity?	
What aspect of God is described in Genesis 1:1–30?	
'If you _ _ _ _ _ _ _ other people when they sin against you, your heavenly Father will also _ _ _ _ _ _ _ you' (Matthew 6:9–15)	
'I, the Lord your God, am a _ _ _ _ _ _ _ God' (Ten Commandments, Exodus 20)	
How many 'persons' are there in the Trinity?	
'You shall have no other _ _ _ _ before me' (Ten Commandments, Exodus 20)	
'For God so loved the world that he gave his one and only _ _ _' (John 3:16)	
'God created _ _ _ _ _ _ _ _ _ _ _, making them to be like himself. He created them male and female' (Genesis 1:27)	

ANSWER KEY

3.1	Name the three persons of the Trinity	1. Father/God 2. Son/Jesus 3. Holy Spirit
3.2	'Jesus answered, "I am the ___ and the _____ and the ____. No one comes to the Father except through me' (John 14:6)	way, truth, life
3.3	'The Word became flesh and made his dwelling among us' (John 1:14). Which person of the Trinity does this describe?	Jesus
3.4	'I and the Father are ___' (John 10:30)	one
3.5	'For our sake he was _____ under Pontius Pilate' (Nicene Creed)	crucified
3.6	At the baptism of Jesus, what form does the Holy Spirit take?	A dove
3.7	Who in the Trinity is the Son?	Jesus
3.8	'We believe in one Lord, Jesus Christ, the only ___ of God' (Nicene Creed)	Son
3.9	During which event in Acts 2 did the Holy Spirit appear in the form of tongues of fire and wind?	Pentecost
3.10	Who in the Trinity is the Father?	God

TRACKER

Quiz	Date	Score
1		
2		
3		
4		
5		
6		

Got it? ☐

3.1	Name the three persons of the Trinity	
3.2	'Jesus answered, "I am the ___ and the _____ and the ____. No one comes to the Father except through me' (John 14:6)	
3.3	'The Word became flesh and made his dwelling among us' (John 1:14). Which person of the Trinity does this describe?	
3.4	'I and the Father are ___' (John 10:30)	
3.5	'For our sake he was _____ under Pontius Pilate' (Nicene Creed)	
3.6	At the baptism of Jesus, what form does the Holy Spirit take?	
3.7	Who in the Trinity is the Son?	
3.8	'We believe in one Lord, Jesus Christ, the only ___ of God' (Nicene Creed)	
3.9	During which event in Acts 2 did the Holy Spirit appear in the form of tongues of fire and wind?	
3.10	Who in the Trinity is the Father?	

'The Word became flesh and made his dwelling among us' (John 1:14). Which person of the Trinity does this describe?	
At the baptism of Jesus, what form does the Holy Spirit take?	
During which event in Acts 2 did the Holy Spirit appear in the form of tongues of fire and wind?	
'Jesus answered, "I am the ___ and the _____ and the ____. No one comes to the Father except through me' (John 14:6)	
'I and the Father are ___' (John 10:30)	
'We believe in one Lord, Jesus Christ, the only ___ of God' (Nicene Creed)	
Who in the Trinity is the Father?	
Name the three persons of the Trinity	
'For our sake he was _____ under Pontius Pilate' (Nicene Creed)	
Who in the Trinity is the Son?	

Who in the Trinity is the Father?	
Name the three persons of the Trinity	
'For our sake he was _ _ _ _ _ _ _ _ _ under Pontius Pilate' (Nicene Creed)	
At the baptism of Jesus, what form does the Holy Spirit take?	
'Jesus answered, "I am the _ _ _ and the _ _ _ _ _ and the _ _ _ _. No one comes to the Father except through me' (John 14:6)	
During which event in Acts 2 did the Holy Spirit appear in the form of tongues of fire and wind?	
Who in the Trinity is the Son?	
'We believe in one Lord, Jesus Christ, the only _ _ _ of God' (Nicene Creed)	
'The Word became flesh and made his dwelling among us' (John 1:14). Which person of the Trinity does this describe?	
'I and the Father are _ _ _' (John 10:30)	

Who in the Trinity is the Father?	
Name the three persons of the Trinity	
'For our sake he was _ _ _ _ _ _ _ _ _ under Pontius Pilate' (Nicene Creed)	
At the baptism of Jesus, what form does the Holy Spirit take?	
'Jesus answered, "I am the _ _ _ and the _ _ _ _ _ and the _ _ _ _. No one comes to the Father except through me' (John 14:6)	
During which event in Acts 2 did the Holy Spirit appear in the form of tongues of fire and wind?	
Who in the Trinity is the Son?	
'We believe in one Lord, Jesus Christ, the only _ _ _ of God' (Nicene Creed)	
'The Word became flesh and made his dwelling among us' (John 1:14). Which person of the Trinity does this describe?	
'I and the Father are _ _ _' (John 10:30)	

Quiz 4: Christian views on creation

ANSWER KEY

4.1	In which book in the Bible are the creation narratives?	Genesis
4.2	According to the Bible, who was the first human created?	Adam
4.3	According to the Bible, how many days did creation take?	Six days (plus one for the day of rest)
4.4	'Be _____ and increase in number' (Genesis 1:28)	fruitful
4.5	What did God do on the seventh day of creation?	He rested
4.6	'In the beginning God created the _____ and the _____' (Genesis 1)	heavens, earth
4.7	Some Christians say the word 'day' doesn't mean 24 hours. What do they believe it means?	An age – a long period of time
4.8	'The earth was formless and empty, darkness was over the surface of the deep, and the _____ __ ___ was hovering over the waters' (Genesis 1:2)	Spirit of God
4.9	'God saw all that he had made, and it was very ____' (Genesis 1:31)	good
4.10	Give two details about how Eve was made, according to the Bible	1. At the same time as Adam (Genesis 1:27) 2. From Adam's rib (Genesis 2:21)

TRACKER

Quiz	Date	Score
1		
2		
3		
4		
5		
6		

Got it? ☐

Quiz 4: Christian views on creation

4.1	In which book in the Bible are the creation narratives?	
4.2	According to the Bible, who was the first human created?	
4.3	According to the Bible, how many days did creation take?	
4.4	'Be _ _ _ _ _ _ _ _ and increase in number' (Genesis 1:28)	
4.5	What did God do on the seventh day of creation?	
4.6	'In the beginning God created the _ _ _ _ _ _ _ and the _ _ _ _ _' (Genesis 1)	
4.7	Some Christians say the word 'day' doesn't mean 24 hours. What do they believe it means?	
4.8	'The earth was formless and empty, darkness was over the surface of the deep, and the _ _ _ _ _ _ _ _ _ _ _ _ was hovering over the waters' (Genesis 1:2)	
4.9	'God saw all that he had made, and it was very _ _ _ _' (Genesis 1:31)	
4.10	Give two details about how Eve was made, according to the Bible	

According to the Bible, how many days did creation take?	
'In the beginning God created the _____ and the _____' (Genesis 1)	
'God saw all that he had made, and it was very ____' (Genesis 1:31)	
According to the Bible, who was the first human created?	
'Be _____ and increase in number' (Genesis 1:28)	
'The earth was formless and empty, darkness was over the surface of the deep, and the _____ __ ___ was hovering over the waters' (Genesis 1:2)	
Give two details about how Eve was made, according to the Bible	
In which book in the Bible are the creation narratives?	
What did God do on the seventh day of creation?	
Some Christians say the word 'day' doesn't mean 24 hours. What do they believe it means?	

Quiz 4: Christian views on creation

Give two details about how Eve was made, according to the Bible	
In which book in the Bible are the creation narratives?	
What did God do on the seventh day of creation?	
'In the beginning God created the _ _ _ _ _ _ _ and the _ _ _ _ _' (Genesis 1)	
According to the Bible, who was the first human created?	
'God saw all that he had made, and it was very _ _ _ _' (Genesis 1:31)	
Some Christians say the word 'day' doesn't mean 24 hours. What do they believe it means?	
'The earth was formless and empty, darkness was over the surface of the deep, and the _ _ _ _ _ _ _ _ _ _ _ was hovering over the waters' (Genesis 1:2)	
According to the Bible, how many days did creation take?	
'Be _ _ _ _ _ _ _ _ and increase in number' (Genesis 1:28)	

Give two details about how Eve was made, according to the Bible	
In which book in the Bible are the creation narratives?	
What did God do on the seventh day of creation?	
'In the beginning God created the _____ and the _____' (Genesis 1)	
According to the Bible, who was the first human created?	
'God saw all that he had made, and it was very ____' (Genesis 1:31)	
Some Christians say the word 'day' doesn't mean 24 hours. What do they believe it means?	
'The earth was formless and empty, darkness was over the surface of the deep, and the _____ __ ___ was hovering over the waters' (Genesis 1:2)	
According to the Bible, how many days did creation take?	
'Be _____ and increase in number' (Genesis 1:28)	

Quiz 5: The problem of evil and suffering

ANSWER KEY

5.1	Why is God being omnipotent an issue in the problem of evil and suffering?	If God was all-powerful he would have the power to stop or prevent suffering
5.2	Why is God being omniscient an issue in the problem of evil and suffering?	If God was all-knowing he would know how to stop or prevent suffering
5.3	Why is God being omnibenevolent an issue in the problem of evil and suffering?	If God was all-loving he wouldn't want humans to suffer
5.4	What is the name of the theory that states God cannot be all three omnis while suffering exists in the world?	The inconsistent triad
5.5	What is the term for evil and suffering caused by humans?	Moral evil
5.6	What is the name given to evil and suffering that exists in nature?	Natural evil
5.7	Who might some Christians attribute the existence of evil and suffering to, instead of God?	Humans or the devil/Satan
5.8	What is the term that describes human beings being able to make decisions without interference from God?	Free will
5.9	According to the Bible, who were the first humans to disobey God, consequently enabling suffering to exist?	Adam and Eve
5.10	How might Christians respond to the problem of evil and suffering?	Pray for those who are suffering; help those who are suffering

TRACKER

Quiz	Date	Score
1		
2		
3		
4		
5		
6		

Got it? ☐

5.1	Why is God being omnipotent an issue in the problem of evil and suffering?	
5.2	Why is God being omniscient an issue in the problem of evil and suffering?	
5.3	Why is God being omnibenevolent an issue in the problem of evil and suffering?	
5.4	What is the name of the theory that states God cannot be all three omnis while suffering exists in the world?	
5.5	What is the term for evil and suffering caused by humans?	
5.6	What is the name given to evil and suffering that exists in nature?	
5.7	Who might some Christians attribute the existence of evil and suffering to, instead of God?	
5.8	What is the term that describes human beings being able to make decisions without interference from God?	
5.9	According to the Bible, who were the first humans to disobey God, consequently enabling suffering to exist?	
5.10	How might Christians respond to the problem of evil and suffering?	

Quiz 5: The problem of evil and suffering

Why is God being omnibenevolent an issue in the problem of evil and suffering?	
What is the name given to evil and suffering that exists in nature?	
According to the Bible, who were the first humans to disobey God, consequently enabling suffering to exist?	
Why is God being omniscient an issue in the problem of evil and suffering?	
What is the name of the theory that states God cannot be all three omnis while suffering exists in the world?	
What is the term that describes human beings being able to make decisions without interference from God?	
How might Christians respond to the problem of evil and suffering?	
Why is God being omnipotent an issue in the problem of evil and suffering?	
What is the term for evil and suffering caused by humans?	
Who might some Christians attribute the existence of evil and suffering to, instead of God?	

How might Christians respond to the problem of evil and suffering?	
Why is God being omnipotent an issue in the problem of evil and suffering?	
What is the term for evil and suffering caused by humans?	
What is the name given to evil and suffering that exists in nature?	
Why is God being omniscient an issue in the problem of evil and suffering?	
According to the Bible, who were the first humans to disobey God, consequently enabling suffering to exist?	
Who might some Christians attribute the existence of evil and suffering to, instead of God?	
What is the term that describes human beings being able to make decisions without interference from God?	
Why is God being omnibenevolent an issue in the problem of evil and suffering?	
What is the name of the theory that states God cannot be all three omnis while suffering exists in the world?	

How might Christians respond to the problem of evil and suffering?	
Why is God being omnipotent an issue in the problem of evil and suffering?	
What is the term for evil and suffering caused by humans?	
What is the name given to evil and suffering that exists in nature?	
Why is God being omniscient an issue in the problem of evil and suffering?	
According to the Bible, who were the first humans to disobey God, consequently enabling suffering to exist?	
Who might some Christians attribute the existence of evil and suffering to, instead of God?	
What is the term that describes human beings being able to make decisions without interference from God?	
Why is God being omnibenevolent an issue in the problem of evil and suffering?	
What is the name of the theory that states God cannot be all three omnis while suffering exists in the world?	

ANSWER KEY

6.1	Some Christians believe that, through their actions in the Garden of Eden, Adam and Eve transmitted a sin to all other human beings. What is the name of this sin?	Original sin
6.2	According to Christianity, who was the snake that tempted Eve in the Garden of Eden?	The devil/Satan (a fallen angel)
6.3	When explaining belief, what is meant by the term 'monotheist'?	Someone who believes in one God
6.4	When explaining belief, what is meant by the term 'agnostic'?	Someone who is unsure about the existence of God
6.5	When explaining belief, what is meant by the term 'atheist'?	Someone who doesn't believe in God
6.6	When explaining belief, what is meant by the term 'theism'?	Belief in God
6.7	What is the name of the event in which Adam and Eve fell from God's grace, by eating the forbidden fruit?	The Fall
6.8	'Lead us not into _____ but deliver us from evil' (Lord's Prayer)	temptation
6.9	Who said: 'Is God willing to prevent evil, but not able? Then he is not omnipotent. Is he able, but not willing? Then he is malevolent. Is he both able and willing? Then whence cometh evil? Is he neither able nor willing? Then why call him God?'	Epicurus
6.10	'There is no one on earth as faithful and good as he is. He worships me and is careful not to do anything evil.' Which Old Testament character is described here?	Job (in Job 1:8)

TRACKER

Quiz	Date	Score
1		
2		
3		
4		
5		
6		

Got it? ☐

6.1	Some Christians believe that, through their actions in the Garden of Eden, Adam and Eve transmitted a sin to all other human beings. What is the name of this sin?	
6.2	According to Christianity, who was the snake that tempted Eve in the Garden of Eden?	
6.3	When explaining belief, what is meant by the term 'monotheist'?	
6.4	When explaining belief, what is meant by the term 'agnostic'?	
6.5	When explaining belief, what is meant by the term 'atheist'?	
6.6	When explaining belief, what is meant by the term 'theism'?	
6.7	What is the name of the event in which Adam and Eve fell from God's grace, by eating the forbidden fruit?	
6.8	'Lead us not into _____ but deliver us from evil' (Lord's Prayer)	
6.9	Who said: 'Is God willing to prevent evil, but not able? Then he is not omnipotent. Is he able, but not willing? Then he is malevolent. Is he both able and willing? Then whence cometh evil? Is he neither able nor willing? Then why call him God?'	
6.10	'There is no one on earth as faithful and good as he is. He worships me and is careful not to do anything evil.' Which Old Testament character is described here?	

When explaining belief, what is meant by the term 'monotheist'?	
When explaining belief, what is meant by the term 'theism'?	
Who said: 'Is God willing to prevent evil, but not able? Then he is not omnipotent. Is he able, but not willing? Then he is malevolent. Is he both able and willing? Then whence cometh evil? Is he neither able nor willing? Then why call him God?'	
According to Christianity, who was the snake that tempted Eve in the Garden of Eden?	
When explaining belief, what is meant by the term 'agnostic'?	
'Lead us not into _ _ _ _ _ _ _ _ _ _ but deliver us from evil' (Lord's Prayer)	
'There is no one on earth as faithful and good as he is. He worships me and is careful not to do anything evil.' Which Old Testament character is described here?	
Some Christians believe that, through their actions in the Garden of Eden, Adam and Eve transmitted a sin to all other human beings. What is the name of this sin?	
When explaining belief, what is meant by the term 'atheist'?	
What is the name of the event in which Adam and Eve fell from God's grace, by eating the forbidden fruit?	

'There is no one on earth as faithful and good as he is. He worships me and is careful not to do anything evil.' Which Old Testament character is described here?	
Some Christians believe that, through their actions in the Garden of Eden, Adam and Eve transmitted a sin to all other human beings. What is the name of this sin?	
When explaining belief, what is meant by the term 'atheist'?	
When explaining belief, what is meant by the term 'theism'?	
According to Christianity, who was the snake that tempted Eve in the Garden of Eden?	
Who said: 'Is God willing to prevent evil, but not able? Then he is not omnipotent. Is he able, but not willing? Then he is malevolent. Is he both able and willing? Then whence cometh evil? Is he neither able nor willing? Then why call him God?'	
What is the name of the event in which Adam and Eve fell from God's grace, by eating the forbidden fruit?	
'Lead us not into _____ but deliver us from evil' (Lord's Prayer)	
When explaining belief, what is meant by the term 'monotheist'?	
When explaining belief, what is meant by the term 'agnostic'?	

'There is no one on earth as faithful and good as he is. He worships me and is careful not to do anything evil.' Which Old Testament character is described here?	
Some Christians believe that, through their actions in the Garden of Eden, Adam and Eve transmitted a sin to all other human beings. What is the name of this sin?	
When explaining belief, what is meant by the term 'atheist'?	
When explaining belief, what is meant by the term 'theism'?	
According to Christianity, who was the snake that tempted Eve in the Garden of Eden?	
Who said: 'Is God willing to prevent evil, but not able? Then he is not omnipotent. Is he able, but not willing? Then he is malevolent. Is he both able and willing? Then whence cometh evil? Is he neither able nor willing? Then why call him God?'	
What is the name of the event in which Adam and Eve fell from God's grace, by eating the forbidden fruit?	
'Lead us not into _____ but deliver us from evil' (Lord's Prayer)	
When explaining belief, what is meant by the term 'monotheist'?	
When explaining belief, what is meant by the term 'agnostic'?	

ANSWER KEY

7.1	'The Word became a human being and, full of grace and truth, lived among us' (John 1:14). Who was this human being?	Jesus Christ
7.2	What was the name of the angel who told Mary she was pregnant?	Gabriel
7.3	What did the angel tell Mary to call her baby?	Jesus
7.4	In which city was Jesus born?	Bethlehem
7.5	How did Mary become pregnant?	By the Holy Spirit (God)
7.6	What was the name of Jesus's earthly father?	Joseph
7.7	Where is the birth of the Messiah predicted in the Bible?	In the Old Testament prophets
7.8	'In the beginning the ____ already existed; the ____ was with God, and the ____ was God' (John 1:1)	Word
7.9	'The Lord God will make him a ____, as his ancestor David was, and he will be the ____ of the descendants of Jacob forever' (Luke 1:32–33)	King
7.10	Which part of the Trinity is the Incarnation?	Son of God/Jesus

TRACKER

Quiz	Date	Score
1		
2		
3		
4		
5		
6		

Got it? ☐

Quiz 7: Jesus – the Incarnation

7.1	'The Word became a human being and, full of grace and truth, lived among us' (John 1:14). Who was this human being?	
7.2	What was the name of the angel who told Mary she was pregnant?	
7.3	What did the angel tell Mary to call her baby?	
7.4	In which city was Jesus born?	
7.5	How did Mary become pregnant?	
7.6	What was the name of Jesus's earthly father?	
7.7	Where is the birth of the Messiah predicted in the Bible?	
7.8	'In the beginning the ____ already existed; the ____ was with God, and the ____ was God' (John 1:1)	
7.9	'The Lord God will make him a ____, as his ancestor David was, and he will be the ____ of the descendants of Jacob forever' (Luke 1:32–33)	
7.10	Which part of the Trinity is the Incarnation?	

Quiz 7: Jesus – the Incarnation

What did the angel tell Mary to call her baby?	
What was the name of Jesus's earthly father?	
'The Lord God will make him a ____, as his ancestor David was, and he will be the ____ of the descendants of Jacob forever' (Luke 1:32–33)	
What was the name of the angel who told Mary she was pregnant?	
In which city was Jesus born?	
'In the beginning the ____ already existed; the ____ was with God, and the ____ was God' (John 1:1)	
Which part of the Trinity is the Incarnation?	
'The Word became a human being and, full of grace and truth, lived among us' (John 1:14). Who was this human being?	
How did Mary become pregnant?	
Where is the birth of the Messiah predicted in the Bible?	

Quiz 7: Jesus – the Incarnation

Which part of the Trinity is the Incarnation?	
'The Word became a human being and, full of grace and truth, lived among us' (John 1:14). Who was this human being?	
How did Mary become pregnant?	
What was the name of Jesus's earthly father?	
What was the name of the angel who told Mary she was pregnant?	
'The Lord God will make him a ____, as his ancestor David was, and he will be the ____ of the descendants of Jacob forever' (Luke 1:32–33)	
Where is the birth of the Messiah predicted in the Bible?	
'In the beginning the ____ already existed; the ____ was with God, and the ____ was God' (John 1:1)	
What did the angel tell Mary to call her baby?	
In which city was Jesus born?	

Which part of the Trinity is the Incarnation?	
'The Word became a human being and, full of grace and truth, lived among us' (John 1:14). Who was this human being?	
How did Mary become pregnant?	
What was the name of Jesus's earthly father?	
What was the name of the angel who told Mary she was pregnant?	
'The Lord God will make him a ____, as his ancestor David was, and he will be the ____ of the descendants of Jacob forever' (Luke 1:32–33)	
Where is the birth of the Messiah predicted in the Bible?	
'In the beginning the ____ already existed; the ____ was with God, and the ____ was God' (John 1:1)	
What did the angel tell Mary to call her baby?	
In which city was Jesus born?	

ANSWER KEY

8.1	How old was Jesus when he ran away from his parents to the temple in Jerusalem?	12
8.2	In which sea did Jesus calm the storm and catch the fish with the disciples?	The Sea of Galilee (also known as Kinneret/Lake Tiberias)
8.3	How many disciples/apostles did Jesus choose to follow him?	12
8.4	What term describes the stories told by Jesus that had a moral or spiritual meaning for his followers to learn from?	Parables
8.5	The healing of the blind man, the feeding of the 5000, the calming of the storm – what are these examples of?	Miracles
8.6	In Matthew 22:36–39, what does Jesus say are the two Great Commandments?	1. 'Love the Lord your God with all your heart and with all your soul and with all your mind' 2. 'Love your neighbour as yourself'
8.7	What is the name given to the collection of Jesus's teachings that includes the Beatitudes?	The Sermon on the Mount
8.8	Why is Jesus referred to as the Saviour?	His death and Resurrection saved humans from their sins so they could have eternal life in heaven with God
8.9	What term describes Christian love?	Agape
8.10	What does the term 'Messiah' mean?	Great leader, anointed one, saviour, liberator

TRACKER

Quiz	Date	Score
1		
2		
3		
4		
5		
6		

Got it? ☐

8.1	How old was Jesus when he ran away from his parents to the temple in Jerusalem?	
8.2	In which sea did Jesus calm the storm and catch the fish with the disciples?	
8.3	How many disciples/apostles did Jesus choose to follow him?	
8.4	What term describes the stories told by Jesus that had a moral or spiritual meaning for his followers to learn from?	
8.5	The healing of the blind man, the feeding of the 5000, the calming of the storm – what are these examples of?	
8.6	In Matthew 22:36–39, what does Jesus say are the two Great Commandments?	
8.7	What is the name given to the collection of Jesus's teachings that includes the Beatitudes?	
8.8	Why is Jesus referred to as the Saviour?	
8.9	What term describes Christian love?	
8.10	What does the term 'Messiah' mean?	

Question	Answer
In Matthew 22:36–39, what does Jesus say are the two Great Commandments?	
How old was Jesus when he ran away from his parents to the temple in Jerusalem?	
How many disciples/apostles did Jesus choose to follow him?	
What is the name given to the collection of Jesus's teachings that includes the Beatitudes?	
The healing of the blind man, the feeding of the 5000, the calming of the storm – what are these examples of?	
Why is Jesus referred to as the Saviour?	
What term describes the stories told by Jesus that had a moral or spiritual meaning for his followers to learn from?	
What does the term 'Messiah' mean?	
In which sea did Jesus calm the storm and catch the fish with the disciples?	
What term describes Christian love?	

How many disciples/apostles did Jesus choose to follow him?	
In Matthew 22:36–39, what does Jesus say are the two Great Commandments?	
What term describes Christian love?	
In which sea did Jesus calm the storm and catch the fish with the disciples?	
What term describes the stories told by Jesus that had a moral or spiritual meaning for his followers to learn from?	
Why is Jesus referred to as the Saviour?	
What does the term 'Messiah' mean?	
How old was Jesus when he ran away from his parents to the temple in Jerusalem?	
The healing of the blind man, the feeding of the 5000, the calming of the storm – what are these examples of?	
What is the name given to the collection of Jesus's teachings that includes the Beatitudes?	

What does the term 'Messiah' mean?	
How old was Jesus when he ran away from his parents to the temple in Jerusalem?	
The healing of the blind man, the feeding of the 5000, the calming of the storm – what are these examples of?	
In Matthew 22:36–39, what does Jesus say are the two Great Commandments?	
In which sea did Jesus calm the storm and catch the fish with the disciples?	
What term describes Christian love?	
What is the name given to the collection of Jesus's teachings that includes the Beatitudes?	
Why is Jesus referred to as the Saviour?	
How many disciples/apostles did Jesus choose to follow him?	
What term describes the stories told by Jesus that had a moral or spiritual meaning for his followers to learn from?	

ANSWER KEY

9.1	What term describes the final meal eaten by Jesus before his Crucifixion?	The Last Supper
9.2	Where was Jesus when he was arrested?	The Garden of Gethsemane
9.3	Who betrayed Jesus by telling the authorities where he would be, for 30 pieces of silver?	Judas Iscariot
9.4	Which leader sent Jesus to be crucified, allowing Barabbas to be freed?	Pontius Pilate
9.5	What was written on the sign placed above Jesus's head on the cross?	'This is Jesus, the King of the Jews'
9.6	What is the name of the place where the Bible says Jesus was crucified?	Golgotha (the place of the skull), outside Jerusalem
9.7	While on the cross, what did Jesus say to the criminal on his right who stood up for him?	'Today you will be with me in paradise'
9.8	What did Jesus call out to God while on the cross?	'My God, my God, why did you abandon me?' ('Eli, Eli, lema sabachthani?')
9.9	Where was Jesus's body put once he had died?	In a tomb cut out of the rock (outside Jerusalem)
9.10	Name one of the women who found the stone had been rolled away and the empty tomb	Mary Magdalene; Joanna; Mary, the mother of James

TRACKER

Quiz	Date	Score
1		
2		
3		
4		
5		
6		

Got it? ☐

9.1	What term describes the final meal eaten by Jesus before his Crucifixion?	
9.2	Where was Jesus when he was arrested?	
9.3	Who betrayed Jesus by telling the authorities where he would be, for 30 pieces of silver?	
9.4	Which leader sent Jesus to be crucified, allowing Barabbas to be freed?	
9.5	What was written on the sign placed above Jesus's head on the cross?	
9.6	What is the name of the place where the Bible says Jesus was crucified?	
9.7	While on the cross, what did Jesus say to the criminal on his right who stood up for him?	
9.8	What did Jesus call out to God while on the cross?	
9.9	Where was Jesus's body put once he had died?	
9.10	Name one of the women who found the stone had been rolled away and the empty tomb	

What is the name of the place where the Bible says Jesus was crucified?	
What term describes the final meal eaten by Jesus before his Crucifixion?	
Who betrayed Jesus by telling the authorities where he would be, for 30 pieces of silver?	
While on the cross, what did Jesus say to the criminal on his right who stood up for him?	
What was written on the sign placed above Jesus's head on the cross?	
What did Jesus call out to God while on the cross?	
Which leader sent Jesus to be crucified, allowing Barabbas to be freed?	
Which leader sent Jesus to be crucified, allowing Barabbas to be freed?	
Where was Jesus when he was arrested?	
Where was Jesus's body put once he had died?	

Who betrayed Jesus by telling the authorities where he would be, for 30 pieces of silver?	
What is the name of the place where the Bible says Jesus was crucified?	
Where was Jesus's body put once he had died?	
Where was Jesus when he was arrested?	
Which leader sent Jesus to be crucified, allowing Barabbas to be freed?	
What did Jesus call out to God while on the cross?	
Name one of the women who found the stone had been rolled away and the empty tomb	
What term describes the final meal eaten by Jesus before his Crucifixion?	
What was written on the sign placed above Jesus's head on the cross?	
While on the cross, what did Jesus say to the criminal on his right who stood up for him?	

Name one of the women who found the stone had been rolled away and the empty tomb	
What term describes the final meal eaten by Jesus before his Crucifixion?	
What was written on the sign placed above Jesus's head on the cross?	
What is the name of the place where the Bible says Jesus was crucified?	
Where was Jesus when he was arrested?	
Where was Jesus's body put once he had died?	
While on the cross, what did Jesus say to the criminal on his right who stood up for him?	
What did Jesus call out to God while on the cross?	
Who betrayed Jesus by telling the authorities where he would be, for 30 pieces of silver?	
Which leader sent Jesus to be crucified, allowing Barabbas to be freed?	

ANSWER KEY

10.1	What did Jesus tell the disciples to do just before the Ascension?	• 'Go, then, to all peoples everywhere and make them my disciples' • ' … baptise them in the name of the Father, the Son, and the Holy Spirit' • ' … teach them to obey everything I have commanded you'
10.2	What is the name of the event in which Jesus gave instructions to the disciples just before the Ascension?	The Great Commission
10.3	Where did Jesus ascend to?	Heaven
10.4	Name one means of salvation	Faith (grace), law (works), Holy Spirit
10.5	What is the correct term for an act against the laws of God?	Sin
10.6	What term is used to describe asking God for forgiveness?	Repentance
10.7	What is the name of the event in which the disciples experienced the Holy Spirit as flames of fire and the ability to speak in tongues?	Pentecost
10.8	'Faith without actions is _____' (James 2:20)	Useless/dead
10.9	'For God so loved the _____ that he gave his one and only ___, that whoever believes in him shall not perish but have _____ life' (John 3:16)	world, Son, eternal
10.10	What does 'salvation' mean in Christianity?	Being 'saved' from sin by restoring the relationship between humans and God

TRACKER

Quiz	Date	Score
1		
2		
3		
4		
5		
6		

Got it? ☐

10.1	What did Jesus tell the disciples to do just before the Ascension?	
10.2	What is the name of the event in which Jesus gave instructions to the disciples just before the Ascension?	
10.3	Where did Jesus ascend to?	
10.4	Name one means of salvation	
10.5	What is the correct term for an act against the laws of God?	
10.6	What term is used to describe asking God for forgiveness?	
10.7	What is the name of the event in which the disciples experienced the Holy Spirit as flames of fire and the ability to speak in tongues?	
10.8	'Faith without actions is _____' (James 2:20)	
10.9	'For God so loved the _____ that he gave his one and only ___, that whoever believes in him shall not perish but have _____ life' (John 3:16)	
10.10	What does 'salvation' mean in Christianity?	

What term is used to describe asking God for forgiveness?	
What did Jesus tell the disciples to do just before the Ascension?	
Where did Jesus ascend to?	
What is the name of the event in which the disciples experienced the Holy Spirit as flames of fire and the ability to speak in tongues?	
What is the correct term for an act against the laws of God?	
'Faith without actions is _____' (James 2:20)	
Name one means of salvation	
What does 'salvation' mean in Christianity?	
What is the name of the event in which Jesus gave instructions to the disciples just before the Ascension?	
'For God so loved the _____ that he gave his one and only ___, that whoever believes in him shall not perish but have _____ life' (John 3:16)	

Where did Jesus ascend to?	
What term is used to describe asking God for forgiveness?	
'For God so loved the _ _ _ _ _ that he gave his one and only _ _ _, that whoever believes in him shall not perish but have _ _ _ _ _ _ _ life' (John 3:16)	
What is the name of the event in which Jesus gave instructions to the disciples just before the Ascension?	
Name one means of salvation	
'Faith without actions is _ _ _ _ _ _ _' (James 2:20)	
What does 'salvation' mean in Christianity?	
What did Jesus tell the disciples to do just before the Ascension?	
What is the correct term for an act against the laws of God?	
What is the name of the event in which the disciples experienced the Holy Spirit as flames of fire and the ability to speak in tongues?	

What does 'salvation' mean in Christianity?	
What did Jesus tell the disciples to do just before the Ascension?	
What is the correct term for an act against the laws of God?	
What term is used to describe asking God for forgiveness?	
What is the name of the event in which Jesus gave instructions to the disciples just before the Ascension?	
'For God so loved the _ _ _ _ _ that he gave his one and only _ _ _, that whoever believes in him shall not perish but have _ _ _ _ _ _ _ life' (John 3:16)	
What is the name of the event in which the disciples experienced the Holy Spirit as flames of fire and the ability to speak in tongues?	
'Faith without actions is _ _ _ _ _ _ _' (James 2:20)	
Where did Jesus ascend to?	
Name one means of salvation	

ANSWER KEY

11.1	What term describes someone coming alive again after death?	Resurrection
11.2	According to the Bible, where will a) good people and b) bad people/ sinners go after death/judgement?	a) Heaven b) Hell
11.3	According to the Bible, e.g. 2 Corinthians 5:10, who will judge humans?	Jesus/God
11.4	In which parable (Matthew 25:31–46) does Jesus describe dividing humans into two groups, based on how they have behaved towards other people?	The Parable of the Sheep and Goats
11.5	'I am the _____ and the life. Those who believe in me will ____, even though they die; and those who live and _____ in me will never die' (John 11:25–26)	resurrection, live, believe
11.6	Why don't some Christians believe in hell?	An all-loving God wouldn't allow people to experience the pain and suffering that hell punishes with
11.7	What term is used by Catholic Christians for the state of purification from sins before going to heaven?	Purgatory
11.8	Some Christians believe in two stages of judgement. When do these happen?	1. When you die 2. Judgement Day (end of the world)
11.9	'There are ____ _____ in my Father's house' (John 14:2–7)	many rooms
11.10	In which book of the Bible are end times described?	Revelation

TRACKER

Quiz	Date	Score
1		
2		
3		
4		
5		
6		

Got it? ☐

11.1	What term describes someone coming alive again after death?	
11.2	According to the Bible, where will a) good people and b) bad people/sinners go after death/judgement?	
11.3	According to the Bible, e.g. 2 Corinthians 5:10, who will judge humans?	
11.4	In which parable (Matthew 25:31–46) does Jesus describe dividing humans into two groups, based on how they have behaved towards other people?	
11.5	'I am the _____ and the life. Those who believe in me will ____, even though they die; and those who live and _____ in me will never die' (John 11:25–26)	
11.6	Why don't some Christians believe in hell?	
11.7	What term is used by Catholic Christians for the state of purification from sins before going to heaven?	
11.8	Some Christians believe in two stages of judgement. When do these happen?	
11.9	'There are ____ _____ in my Father's house' (John 14:2–7)	
11.10	In which book of the Bible are end times described?	

Why don't some Christians believe in hell?	
Why don't some Christians believe in hell?	
According to the Bible, e.g. 2 Corinthians 5:10, who will judge humans?	
What term is used by Catholic Christians for the state of purification from sins before going to heaven?	
'I am the _ _ _ _ _ _ _ _ _ _ _ and the life. Those who believe in me will _ _ _ _, even though they die; and those who live and _ _ _ _ _ _ _ in me will never die' (John 11:25–26)	
Some Christians believe in two stages of judgement. When do these happen?	
In which parable (Matthew 25:31–46) does Jesus describe dividing humans into two groups, based on how they have behaved towards other people?	
In which book of the Bible are end times described?	
According to the Bible, where will a) good people and b) bad people/sinners go after death/judgement?	
'There are _ _ _ _ _ _ _ _ _ in my Father's house' (John 14:2–7)	

According to the Bible, e.g. 2 Corinthians 5:10, who will judge humans?	
Why don't some Christians believe in hell?	
'There are ____ _____ in my Father's house' (John 14:2–7)	
According to the Bible, where will a) good people and b) bad people/sinners go after death/judgement?	
In which parable (Matthew 25:31–46) does Jesus describe dividing humans into two groups, based on how they have behaved towards other people?	
Some Christians believe in two stages of judgement. When do these happen?	
In which book of the Bible are end times described?	
What term describes someone coming alive again after death?	
'I am the _____ and the life. Those who believe in me will ____, even though they die; and those who live and _____ in me will never die' (John 11:25–26)	
What term is used by Catholic Christians for the state of purification from sins before going to heaven?	

In which book of the Bible are end times described?	
What term describes someone coming alive again after death?	
'I am the _____ and the life. Those who believe in me will _____, even though they die; and those who live and _____ in me will never die' (John 11:25–26)	
Why don't some Christians believe in hell?	
According to the Bible, where will a) good people and b) bad people/sinners go after death/judgement?	
'There are _____ _____ in my Father's house' (John 14:2–7)	
What term is used by Catholic Christians for the state of purification from sins before going to heaven?	
Some Christians believe in two stages of judgement. When do these happen?	
According to the Bible, e.g. 2 Corinthians 5:10, who will judge humans?	
In which parable (Matthew 25:31–46) does Jesus describe dividing humans into two groups, based on how they have behaved towards other people?	

Quiz 12: Life after death 2

ANSWER KEY

12.1	What do most Christians believe heaven is?	A place/state of being after death, with God, for eternity
12.2	According to the Bible, what are those who go to hell thrown into?	An eternal furnace of fire
12.3	What two 'types' of body does 1 Corinthians 15:42–49 describe?	Physical and spiritual
12.4	According to biblical imagery, what will Jesus be sat upon at judgement?	A throne
12.5	What is the term for the study of life after death and judgement?	Eschatology
12.6	What is the meaning of atonement?	At-one-ment – humans restoring their relationship with God, enabled by the death and Resurrection of Jesus
12.7	'He will come again in glory to _ _ _ _ _ the living and the dead, and his kingdom will have no end' (Nicene Creed)	judge
12.8	'I believe in the Holy Spirit, the holy catholic Church, the communion of saints, the forgiveness of sins, the _ _ _ _ _ _ _ _ _ _ _ _ of the body, and the life everlasting' (Apostles' Creed)	resurrection
12.9	According to 1 Corinthians 15:51–52, what instrument will signify the final Resurrection?	Trumpet
12.10	Which Greek word means the second coming of Jesus on earth?	Parousia

TRACKER

Quiz	Date	Score
1		
2		
3		
4		
5		
6		

Got it? ☐

12.1	What do most Christians believe heaven is?	
12.2	According to the Bible, what are those who go to hell thrown into?	
12.3	What two 'types' of body does 1 Corinthians 15:42–49 describe?	
12.4	According to biblical imagery, what will Jesus be sat upon at judgement?	
12.5	What is the term for the study of life after death and judgement?	
12.6	What is the meaning of atonement?	
12.7	'He will come again in glory to _ _ _ _ _ the living and the dead, and his kingdom will have no end' (Nicene Creed)	
12.8	'I believe in the Holy Spirit, the holy catholic Church, the communion of saints, the forgiveness of sins, the _ _ _ _ _ _ _ _ _ _ _ _ of the body, and the life everlasting' (Apostles' Creed)	
12.9	According to 1 Corinthians 15:51–52, what instrument will signify the final Resurrection?	
12.10	Which Greek word means the second coming of Jesus on earth?	

What is the meaning of atonement?	
What do most Christians believe heaven is?	
What two 'types' of body does 1 Corinthians 15:42–49 describe?	
'He will come again in glory to _____ the living and the dead, and his kingdom will have no end' (Nicene Creed)	
What is the term for the study of life after death and judgement?	
'I believe in the Holy Spirit, the holy catholic Church, the communion of saints, the forgiveness of sins, the _____ of the body, and the life everlasting' (Apostles' Creed)	
According to biblical imagery, what will Jesus be sat upon at judgement?	
Which Greek word means the second coming of Jesus on earth?	
According to the Bible, what are those who go to hell thrown into?	
According to 1 Corinthians 15:51–52, what instrument will signify the final Resurrection?	

What two 'types' of body does 1 Corinthians 15:42–49 describe?	
What is the meaning of atonement?	
According to 1 Corinthians 15:51–52, what instrument will signify the final Resurrection?	
According to the Bible, what are those who go to hell thrown into?	
According to biblical imagery, what will Jesus be sat upon at judgement?	
'I believe in the Holy Spirit, the holy catholic Church, the communion of saints, the forgiveness of sins, the _____ of the body, and the life everlasting' (Apostles' Creed)	
Which Greek word means the second coming of Jesus on earth?	
What do most Christians believe heaven is?	
What is the term for the study of life after death and judgement?	
'He will come again in glory to _____ the living and the dead, and his kingdom will have no end' (Nicene Creed)	

Which Greek word means the second coming of Jesus on earth?	
What do most Christians believe heaven is?	
What is the term for the study of life after death and judgement?	
What is the meaning of atonement?	
According to the Bible, what are those who go to hell thrown into?	
According to 1 Corinthians 15:51–52, what instrument will signify the final Resurrection?	
'He will come again in glory to _____ the living and the dead, and his kingdom will have no end' (Nicene Creed)	
'I believe in the Holy Spirit, the holy catholic Church, the communion of saints, the forgiveness of sins, the _____ of the body, and the life everlasting' (Apostles' Creed)	
What two 'types' of body does 1 Corinthians 15:42–49 describe?	
According to biblical imagery, what will Jesus be sat upon at judgement?	

Practices

ANSWER KEY

13.1	What is a sacrament?	An outer display of an inner belief
13.2	Give another name for the Eucharist	Mass, Holy Communion, the Lord's Supper, breaking of bread, Divine Liturgy
13.3	Which event is re-enacted/ remembered at the Eucharist?	The Last Supper
13.4	Which sacrament did Jesus tell the disciples to perform at the Great Commission?	Baptism (in the name of the Father, Son and Holy Spirit) – Matthew 28:19
13.5	What term describes the Catholic belief that the bread becomes the body and the wine becomes the blood of Jesus?	Transubstantiation
13.6	Who baptised Jesus and where were they?	John the Baptist at the River Jordan
13.7	How many sacraments are there in the Catholic Church?	Seven
13.8	Why don't some Christians perform infant baptism?	They believe it should be the person's choice and infants are too young to make that decision
13.9	Give one of the main reasons why some Christians have baptisms	To welcome someone into the Church family; to wash away their sins; to show a commitment to Christianity; Jesus was baptised; Jesus told people to baptise; to have a new life with Jesus
13.10	What did Jesus tell the disciples to remember him by at the Last Supper?	Bread (his body) and wine (his blood)

TRACKER

Quiz	Date	Score
1		
2		
3		
4		
5		
6		

Got it? ☐

13.1	What is a sacrament?	
13.2	Give another name for the Eucharist	
13.3	Which event is re-enacted/ remembered at the Eucharist?	
13.4	Which sacrament did Jesus tell the disciples to perform at the Great Commission?	
13.5	What term describes the Catholic belief that the bread becomes the body and the wine becomes the blood of Jesus?	
13.6	Who baptised Jesus and where were they?	
13.7	How many sacraments are there in the Catholic Church?	
13.8	Why don't some Christians perform infant baptism?	
13.9	Give one of the main reasons why some Christians have baptisms	
13.10	What did Jesus tell the disciples to remember him by at the Last Supper?	

Which event is re-enacted/remembered at the Eucharist?	
Who baptised Jesus and where were they?	
Give one of the main reasons why some Christians have baptisms	
Give another name for the Eucharist	
Which sacrament did Jesus tell the disciples to perform at the Great Commission?	
Why don't some Christians perform infant baptism?	
What did Jesus tell the disciples to remember him by at the Last Supper?	
What is a sacrament?	
What term describes the Catholic belief that the bread becomes the body and the wine becomes the blood of Jesus?	
How many sacraments are there in the Catholic Church?	

What did Jesus tell the disciples to remember him by at the Last Supper?	
What is a sacrament?	
What term describes the Catholic belief that the bread becomes the body and the wine becomes the blood of Jesus?	
Who baptised Jesus and where were they?	
Give another name for the Eucharist	
Give one of the main reasons why some Christians have baptisms	
How many sacraments are there in the Catholic Church?	
Why don't some Christians perform infant baptism?	
Which event is re-enacted/remembered at the Eucharist?	
Which sacrament did Jesus tell the disciples to perform at the Great Commission?	

Who baptised Jesus and where were they?	
What is a sacrament?	
Which event is re-enacted/remembered at the Eucharist?	
How many sacraments are there in the Catholic Church?	
What term describes the Catholic belief that the bread becomes the body and the wine becomes the blood of Jesus?	
Why don't some Christians perform infant baptism?	
Which sacrament did Jesus tell the disciples to perform at the Great Commission?	
What did Jesus tell the disciples to remember him by at the Last Supper?	
Give another name for the Eucharist	
Give one of the main reasons why some Christians have baptisms	

Which event is re-enacted/remembered at the Eucharist?	
Who baptised Jesus and where were they?	
Give one of the main reasons why some Christians have baptisms	
Give another name for the Eucharist	
Which sacrament did Jesus tell the disciples to perform at the Great Commission?	
Why don't some Christians perform infant baptism?	
What did Jesus tell the disciples to remember him by at the Last Supper?	
What is a sacrament?	
What term describes the Catholic belief that the bread becomes the body and the wine becomes the blood of Jesus?	
How many sacraments are there in the Catholic Church?	

What did Jesus tell the disciples to remember him by at the Last Supper?	
What is a sacrament?	
What term describes the Catholic belief that the bread becomes the body and the wine becomes the blood of Jesus?	
Who baptised Jesus and where were they?	
Give another name for the Eucharist	
Give one of the main reasons why some Christians have baptisms	
How many sacraments are there in the Catholic Church?	
Why don't some Christians perform infant baptism?	
Which event is re-enacted/remembered at the Eucharist?	
Which sacrament did Jesus tell the disciples to perform at the Great Commission?	

ANSWER KEY

14.1	Which sacraments do the 39 Articles of Religion in the Church of England support?	Baptism and the Lord's Supper (Eucharist)
14.2	'"This is my body, which is for you. __ ____ __ _____ __ __." In the same way, after the supper he took the cup and said, 'This cup is God's new covenant, sealed with my blood. Whenever you drink it, __ ____ __ _____ __ __"' (1 Corinthians 11:23–26)	Do this in memory of me
14.3	Why do Catholic and Orthodox Christians believe infant baptism is important?	It removes original sin
14.4	What sign is made on the baby's forehead with holy water during infant baptism?	The sign of the cross
14.5	What do some Christian denominations give the baby as a symbol of their new life?	A candle (lit from the Paschal candle)
14.6	During baptism, most priests/leaders say, 'I baptise you in the name of the _____, and of the ___, and of the ____ _____'	Father, Son, Holy Spirit
14.7	What is another name for adult baptism, when people decide for themselves to join the Church?	Believer's baptism
14.8	Name a mainstream Christian denomination that has no sacraments	Salvation Army, Quakers
14.9	Name the sacraments that Catholic Christians follow	Baptism, confirmation, Holy Communion, marriage, holy orders, reconciliation, anointing of the sick
14.10	Name a mainstream Christian denomination that doesn't baptise babies, but does baptise adults	Baptists

TRACKER

Quiz	Date	Score
1		
2		
3		
4		
5		
6		

Got it? ☐

14.1	Which sacraments do the 39 Articles of Religion in the Church of England support?	
14.2	'"This is my body, which is for you. __ ____ __ _____ __ __." In the same way, after the supper he took the cup and said, 'This cup is God's new covenant, sealed with my blood. Whenever you drink it, __ ____ __ _____ __ __"' (1 Corinthians 11:23–26)	
14.3	Why do Catholic and Orthodox Christians believe infant baptism is important?	
14.4	What sign is made on the baby's forehead with holy water during infant baptism?	
14.5	What do some Christian denominations give the baby as a symbol of their new life?	
14.6	During baptism, most priests/ leaders say, 'I baptise you in the name of the _____, and of the ___, and of the ____ _____'	
14.7	What is another name for adult baptism, when people decide for themselves to join the Church?	
14.8	Name a mainstream Christian denomination that has no sacraments	
14.9	Name the sacraments that Catholic Christians follow	
14.10	Name a mainstream Christian denomination that doesn't baptise babies, but does baptise adults	

Why do Catholic and Orthodox Christians believe infant baptism is important?	
During baptism, most priests/leaders say, 'I baptise you in the name of the _ _ _ _ _ _, and of the _ _ _, and of the _ _ _ _ _ _ _ _ _'	
Name the sacraments that Catholic Christians follow	
'"This is my body, which is for you. _ _ _ _ _ _ _ _ _ _ _ _ _ _ _ _ _ _." In the same way, after the supper he took the cup and said, 'This cup is God's new covenant, sealed with my blood. Whenever you drink it, _ _ _ _ _ _ _ _ _ _ _ _ _ _ _ _ _"' (1 Corinthians 11:23–26)	
What sign is made on the baby's forehead with holy water during infant baptism?	
Name a mainstream Christian denomination that has no sacraments	
Name a mainstream Christian denomination that doesn't baptise babies, but does baptise adults	
Which sacraments do the 39 Articles of Religion in the Church of England support?	
What do some Christian denominations give the baby as a symbol of their new life?	
What is another name for adult baptism, when people decide for themselves to join the Church?	

Quiz 14: Sacraments 2

Name a mainstream Christian denomination that doesn't baptise babies, but does baptise adults	
Which sacraments do the 39 Articles of Religion in the Church of England support?	
What do some Christian denominations give the baby as a symbol of their new life?	
During baptism, most priests/leaders say, 'I baptise you in the name of the _____, and of the ___, and of the ____ _____'	
'"This is my body, which is for you. __ ____ __ _____ __ __." In the same way, after the supper he took the cup and said, 'This cup is God's new covenant, sealed with my blood. Whenever you drink it, __ ____ __ _____ __ __"' (1 Corinthians 11:23–26)	
Name the sacraments that Catholic Christians follow	
What is another name for adult baptism, when people decide for themselves to join the Church?	
Name a mainstream Christian denomination that has no sacraments	
Why do Catholic and Orthodox Christians believe infant baptism is important?	
What sign is made on the baby's forehead with holy water during infant baptism?	

During baptism, most priests/leaders say, 'I baptise you in the name of the _____, and of the ___, and of the ____ _____'	
Which sacraments do the 39 Articles of Religion in the Church of England support?	
Why do Catholic and Orthodox Christians believe infant baptism is important?	
What is another name for adult baptism, when people decide for themselves to join the Church?	
What do some Christian denominations give the baby as a symbol of their new life?	
Name a mainstream Christian denomination that has no sacraments	
What sign is made on the baby's forehead with holy water during infant baptism?	
Name a mainstream Christian denomination that doesn't baptise babies, but does baptise adults	
'"This is my body, which is for you. __ ____ __ _____ __ __." In the same way, after the supper he took the cup and said, 'This cup is God's new covenant, sealed with my blood. Whenever you drink it, __ ____ __ _____ __ __"' (1 Corinthians 11:23–26)	
Name the sacraments that Catholic Christians follow	

Why do Catholic and Orthodox Christians believe infant baptism is important?	
During baptism, most priests/leaders say, 'I baptise you in the name of the _____, and of the ___, and of the ____ _____'	
Name the sacraments that Catholic Christians follow	
'"This is my body, which is for you. __ ____ __ _____ __ __." In the same way, after the supper he took the cup and said, 'This cup is God's new covenant, sealed with my blood. Whenever you drink it, __ ____ __ _____ __ __."' (1 Corinthians 11:23–26)	
What sign is made on the baby's forehead with holy water during infant baptism?	
Name a mainstream Christian denomination that has no sacraments	
Name a mainstream Christian denomination that doesn't baptise babies, but does baptise adults	
Which sacraments do the 39 Articles of Religion in the Church of England support?	
What do some Christian denominations give the baby as a symbol of their new life?	
What is another name for adult baptism, when people decide for themselves to join the Church?	

Name a mainstream Christian denomination that doesn't baptise babies, but does baptise adults	
Which sacraments do the 39 Articles of Religion in the Church of England support?	
What do some Christian denominations give the baby as a symbol of their new life?	
During baptism, most priests/leaders say, 'I baptise you in the name of the _ _ _ _ _ _, and of the _ _ _, and of the _ _ _ _ _ _ _ _ _ _'	
'"This is my body, which is for you. _ _ _ _ _ _ _ _ _ _ _ _ _ _ _ _ _ _." In the same way, after the supper he took the cup and said, 'This cup is God's new covenant, sealed with my blood. Whenever you drink it, _ _ _ _ _ _ _ _ _ _ _ _ _ _ _ _"' (1 Corinthians 11:23–26)	
Name the sacraments that Catholic Christians follow	
What is another name for adult baptism, when people decide for themselves to join the Church?	
Name a mainstream Christian denomination that has no sacraments	
Why do Catholic and Orthodox Christians believe infant baptism is important?	
What sign is made on the baby's forehead with holy water during infant baptism?	

ANSWER KEY

15.1	What is prayer?	Talking/communicating with God
15.2	What type of prayer is spontaneous and made up by the person praying?	Informal prayer
15.3	What is formal, set prayer?	A prayer where the words have already been decided/have already been written and used multiple times
15.4	Name an example of a set prayer	The Lord's Prayer
15.5	How do Orthodox Christians pray?	Standing up
15.6	What object might Catholic Christians hold in their hands while they pray?	A rosary
15.7	'Our Father in _____, hallowed be your name, your kingdom come, your will be done, on earth as in heaven. Give us today our daily _____ ... ' (Lord's Prayer, contemporary)	heaven, bread
15.8	Name one of the main focuses of prayer	Praise to Jesus/God; thanksgiving; confession (asking for forgiveness of sins); intercession (praying for others); petition (asking for something)
15.9	'_____ us our sins as we _____ those who sin against us. Lead us not into temptation but deliver us from ____. For the kingdom, the power, and the glory are yours now and for ever. Amen' (Lord's Prayer, contemporary)	forgive, forgive, evil
15.10	Where did the Lord's Prayer originate?	From Jesus, when he was asked how people should pray (Luke 11:1–4 and Matthew 6:5–15)

TRACKER

Quiz	Date	Score
1		
2		
3		
4		
5		
6		

Got it? ☐

Quiz 15: Prayer

15.1	What is prayer?	
15.2	What type of prayer is spontaneous and made up by the person praying?	
15.3	What is formal, set prayer?	
15.4	Name an example of a set prayer	
15.5	How do Orthodox Christians pray?	
15.6	What object might Catholic Christians hold in their hands while they pray?	
15.7	'Our Father in _____, hallowed be your name, your kingdom come, your will be done, on earth as in heaven. Give us today our daily _____ … ' (Lord's Prayer, contemporary)	
15.8	Name one of the main focuses of prayer	
15.9	'_____ us our sins as we _____ those who sin against us. Lead us not into temptation but deliver us from ____. For the kingdom, the power, and the glory are yours now and for ever. Amen' (Lord's Prayer, contemporary)	
15.10	Where did the Lord's Prayer originate?	

What is formal, set prayer?	
What object might Catholic Christians hold in their hands while they pray?	
'_____ us our sins as we _____ those who sin against us. Lead us not into temptation but deliver us from ____. For the kingdom, the power, and the glory are yours now and for ever. Amen' (Lord's Prayer, contemporary)	
What type of prayer is spontaneous and made up by the person praying?	
Name an example of a set prayer	
Name one of the main focuses of prayer	
Where did the Lord's Prayer originate?	
What is prayer?	
How do Orthodox Christians pray?	
'Our Father in _____, hallowed be your name, your kingdom come, your will be done, on earth as in heaven. Give us today our daily _____ ...' (Lord's Prayer, contemporary)	

Where did the Lord's Prayer originate?	
What is prayer?	
How do Orthodox Christians pray?	
What object might Catholic Christians hold in their hands while they pray?	
What type of prayer is spontaneous and made up by the person praying?	
'_ _ _ _ _ _ _ us our sins as we _ _ _ _ _ _ _ those who sin against us. Lead us not into temptation but deliver us from _ _ _ _. For the kingdom, the power, and the glory are yours now and for ever. Amen' (Lord's Prayer, contemporary)	
'Our Father in _ _ _ _ _ _, hallowed be your name, your kingdom come, your will be done, on earth as in heaven. Give us today our daily _ _ _ _ _ … ' (Lord's Prayer, contemporary)	
Name one of the main focuses of prayer	
What is formal, set prayer?	
Name an example of a set prayer	

What object might Catholic Christians hold in their hands while they pray?	
What is prayer?	
What is formal, set prayer?	
'Our Father in _ _ _ _ _ _, hallowed be your name, your kingdom come, your will be done, on earth as in heaven. Give us today our daily _ _ _ _ _ … ' (Lord's Prayer, contemporary)	
How do Orthodox Christians pray?	
Name one of the main focuses of prayer	
Name an example of a set prayer	
Where did the Lord's Prayer originate?	
What type of prayer is spontaneous and made up by the person praying?	
'_ _ _ _ _ _ _ us our sins as we _ _ _ _ _ _ _ those who sin against us. Lead us not into temptation but deliver us from _ _ _ _. For the kingdom, the power, and the glory are yours now and for ever. Amen' (Lord's Prayer, contemporary)	

Quiz 15: Prayer

What is formal, set prayer?	
What object might Catholic Christians hold in their hands while they pray?	
'_____ us our sins as we _____ those who sin against us. Lead us not into temptation but deliver us from ____. For the kingdom, the power, and the glory are yours now and for ever. Amen' (Lord's Prayer, contemporary)	
What type of prayer is spontaneous and made up by the person praying?	
Name an example of a set prayer	
Name one of the main focuses of prayer	
Where did the Lord's Prayer originate?	
What is prayer?	
How do Orthodox Christians pray?	
'Our Father in _____, hallowed be your name, your kingdom come, your will be done, on earth as in heaven. Give us today our daily _____ ...' (Lord's Prayer, contemporary)	

Where did the Lord's Prayer originate?	
What is prayer?	
How do Orthodox Christians pray?	
What object might Catholic Christians hold in their hands while they pray?	
What type of prayer is spontaneous and made up by the person praying?	
'_____ us our sins as we _____ those who sin against us. Lead us not into temptation but deliver us from ____. For the kingdom, the power, and the glory are yours now and for ever. Amen' (Lord's Prayer, contemporary)	
'Our Father in _____, hallowed be your name, your kingdom come, your will be done, on earth as in heaven. Give us today our daily _____ ... ' (Lord's Prayer, contemporary)	
Name one of the main focuses of prayer	
What is formal, set prayer?	
Name an example of a set prayer	

ANSWER KEY

16.1	What is the purpose of Christian worship?	To show respect to God; to follow Christian traditions; to show commitment; to praise God; to develop a person's relationship with God
16.2	What is liturgical worship?	A set service that follows a pre-planned structure
16.3	Why is Sunday the main day of worship for Christians?	The Ten Commandments says to remember the Sabbath day (interpreted as the seventh day for Christians)
16.4	What is informal worship?	A charismatic, spontaneous style of worship that has no pre-planned, set style
16.5	Name one possible feature of liturgical worship	Bible reading, singing of hymns/songs, Eucharist, set prayers, chanting
16.6	Why might a Christian use a Bible in private worship?	For guidance from God; to read God's word; for inspiration; for support
16.7	Which Christian denomination mainly worships in silence without any set liturgy?	Quakers (Society of Friends)
16.8	What is the name of the book used by Anglican Christians that contains set prayers?	Book of Common Prayer
16.9	Name one possible feature of informal worship	Dancing, singing, speaking in tongues, clapping, raising hands in the air
16.10	Which part of the Trinity is associated with the divine presence during informal worship?	The Holy Spirit

TRACKER

Quiz	Date	Score
1		
2		
3		
4		
5		
6		

Got it? ☐

Quiz 16: Worship

16.1	What is the purpose of Christian worship?	
16.2	What is liturgical worship?	
16.3	Why is Sunday the main day of worship for Christians?	
16.4	What is informal worship?	
16.5	Name one possible feature of liturgical worship	
16.6	Why might a Christian use a Bible in private worship?	
16.7	Which Christian denomination mainly worships in silence without any set liturgy?	
16.8	What is the name of the book used by Anglican Christians that contains set prayers?	
16.9	Name one possible feature of informal worship	
16.10	Which part of the Trinity is associated with the divine presence during informal worship?	

Quiz 16: Worship

Why is Sunday the main day of worship for Christians?	
Why might a Christian use a Bible in private worship?	
Name one possible feature of informal worship	
What is liturgical worship?	
What is informal worship?	
What is the name of the book used by Anglican Christians that contains set prayers?	
Which part of the Trinity is associated with the divine presence during informal worship?	
What is the purpose of Christian worship?	
Name one possible feature of liturgical worship	
Which Christian denomination mainly worships in silence without any set liturgy?	

Which part of the Trinity is associated with the divine presence during informal worship?	
What is the purpose of Christian worship?	
Name one possible feature of liturgical worship	
Why might a Christian use a Bible in private worship?	
What is liturgical worship?	
Name one possible feature of informal worship	
Which Christian denomination mainly worships in silence without any set liturgy?	
What is the name of the book used by Anglican Christians that contains set prayers?	
Why is Sunday the main day of worship for Christians?	
What is informal worship?	

Why might a Christian use a Bible in private worship?	
What is the purpose of Christian worship?	
Why is Sunday the main day of worship for Christians?	
Which Christian denomination mainly worships in silence without any set liturgy?	
Name one possible feature of liturgical worship	
What is the name of the book used by Anglican Christians that contains set prayers?	
What is informal worship?	
Which part of the Trinity is associated with the divine presence during informal worship?	
What is liturgical worship?	
Name one possible feature of informal worship	

Why is Sunday the main day of worship for Christians?	
Why might a Christian use a Bible in private worship?	
Name one possible feature of informal worship	
What is liturgical worship?	
What is informal worship?	
What is the name of the book used by Anglican Christians that contains set prayers?	
Which part of the Trinity is associated with the divine presence during informal worship?	
What is the purpose of Christian worship?	
Name one possible feature of liturgical worship	
Which Christian denomination mainly worships in silence without any set liturgy?	

Which part of the Trinity is associated with the divine presence during informal worship?	
What is the purpose of Christian worship?	
Name one possible feature of liturgical worship	
Why might a Christian use a Bible in private worship?	
What is liturgical worship?	
Name one possible feature of informal worship	
Which Christian denomination mainly worships in silence without any set liturgy?	
What is the name of the book used by Anglican Christians that contains set prayers?	
Why is Sunday the main day of worship for Christians?	
What is informal worship?	

Quiz 17: Pilgrimage 1

ANSWER KEY

Check your specification for the places of pilgrimage that you need to study

17.1	What is a pilgrimage?	A religious or spiritual journey to a place of importance
17.2	Why do Christians go on a pilgrimage?	To see a special place associated with Christianity; for healing; to see places mentioned in the Bible; to bring them closer to Jesus/God
17.3	What might a Christian do when they arrive at the place of pilgrimage?	Pray, perform acts of worship, kiss/touch a relic, collect something, e.g. water from a spring
17.4	Which town would Christian pilgrims visit to see the place of Jesus's birth?	Bethlehem
17.5	Which city would Christians visit to see where Jesus went to the temple, where Jesus was crucified and the tomb Jesus was buried in?	Jerusalem
17.6	Why is Rome an important place of pilgrimage for some Christians?	It is where the Pope lives (The Vatican); it is where St Peter and St Paul were martyred; it is the centre of the Catholic Church; it is significant in the history of Christianity
17.7	What is the name of the French, ecumenical monastic order popular with Christian pilgrims?	Taizé
17.8	What do pilgrims do in Taizé?	Meditate, pray, chant, worship by candlelight, pray with the monks, sit in silence
17.9	Who did Richeldis de Faverches see in a vision at Walsingham?	The Virgin Mary
17.10	Richeldis de Faverches believed she visited an important place of Christian pilgrimage in her vision. What nickname given to Walsingham references this place?	The Nazareth of England

TRACKER

Quiz	Date	Score
1		
2		
3		
4		
5		
6		

Got it? ☐

17.1	What is a pilgrimage?	
17.2	Why do Christians go on a pilgrimage?	
17.3	What might a Christian do when they arrive at the place of pilgrimage?	
17.4	Which town would Christian pilgrims visit to see the place of Jesus's birth?	
17.5	Which city would Christians visit to see where Jesus went to the temple, where Jesus was crucified and the tomb Jesus was buried in?	
17.6	Why is Rome an important place of pilgrimage for some Christians?	
17.7	What is the name of the French, ecumenical monastic order popular with Christian pilgrims?	
17.8	What do pilgrims do in Taizé?	
17.9	Who did Richeldis de Faverches see in a vision at Walsingham?	
17.10	Richeldis de Faverches believed she visited an important place of Christian pilgrimage in her vision. What nickname given to Walsingham references this place?	

What might a Christian do when they arrive at the place of pilgrimage?	
Why is Rome an important place of pilgrimage for some Christians?	
Who did Richeldis de Faverches see in a vision at Walsingham?	
Why do Christians go on a pilgrimage?	
Which town would Christian pilgrims visit to see the place of Jesus's birth?	
What do pilgrims do in Taizé?	
Richeldis de Faverches believed she visited an important place of Christian pilgrimage in her vision. What nickname given to Walsingham references this place?	
What is a pilgrimage?	
Which city would Christians visit to see where Jesus went to the temple, where Jesus was crucified and the tomb Jesus was buried in?	
What is the name of the French, ecumenical monastic order popular with Christian pilgrims?	

Richeldis de Faverches believed she visited an important place of Christian pilgrimage in her vision. What nickname given to Walsingham references this place?	
What is a pilgrimage?	
Which city would Christians visit to see where Jesus went to the temple, where Jesus was crucified and the tomb Jesus was buried in?	
Why is Rome an important place of pilgrimage for some Christians?	
Why do Christians go on a pilgrimage?	
Who did Richeldis de Faverches see in a vision at Walsingham?	
What is the name of the French, ecumenical monastic order popular with Christian pilgrims?	
What do pilgrims do in Taizé?	
What might a Christian do when they arrive at the place of pilgrimage?	
Which town would Christian pilgrims visit to see the place of Jesus's birth?	

Why is Rome an important place of pilgrimage for some Christians?	
What is a pilgrimage?	
What might a Christian do when they arrive at the place of pilgrimage?	
What is the name of the French, ecumenical monastic order popular with Christian pilgrims?	
Which city would Christians visit to see where Jesus went to the temple, where Jesus was crucified and the tomb Jesus was buried in?	
What do pilgrims do in Taizé?	
Which town would Christian pilgrims visit to see the place of Jesus's birth?	
Richeldis de Faverches believed she visited an important place of Christian pilgrimage in her vision. What nickname given to Walsingham references this place?	
Why do Christians go on a pilgrimage?	
Who did Richeldis de Faverches see in a vision at Walsingham?	

What might a Christian do when they arrive at the place of pilgrimage?	
Why is Rome an important place of pilgrimage for some Christians?	
Who did Richeldis de Faverches see in a vision at Walsingham?	
Why do Christians go on a pilgrimage?	
Which town would Christian pilgrims visit to see the place of Jesus's birth?	
What do pilgrims do in Taizé?	
Richeldis de Faverches believed she visited an important place of Christian pilgrimage in her vision. What nickname given to Walsingham references this place?	
What is a pilgrimage?	
Which city would Christians visit to see where Jesus went to the temple, where Jesus was crucified and the tomb Jesus was buried in?	
What is the name of the French, ecumenical monastic order popular with Christian pilgrims?	

Richeldis de Faverches believed she visited an important place of Christian pilgrimage in her vision. What nickname given to Walsingham references this place?	
What is a pilgrimage?	
Which city would Christians visit to see where Jesus went to the temple, where Jesus was crucified and the tomb Jesus was buried in?	
Why is Rome an important place of pilgrimage for some Christians?	
Why do Christians go on a pilgrimage?	
Who did Richeldis de Faverches see in a vision at Walsingham?	
What is the name of the French, ecumenical monastic order popular with Christian pilgrims?	
What do pilgrims do in Taizé?	
What might a Christian do when they arrive at the place of pilgrimage?	
Which town would Christian pilgrims visit to see the place of Jesus's birth?	

ANSWER KEY

Check your specification for the places of pilgrimage that you need to study

18.1	In which country is Lourdes?	France
18.2	What is the name of the girl who had visions at Lourdes?	Bernadette Soubirous
18.3	Who did the girl have visions of?	The Virgin Mary
18.4	Why do pilgrims visit Lourdes?	To be healed or to accompany someone who hopes to be healed; to visit the Grotto where Mary appeared; to pray (using the rosary); to take part in processions and Mass; to confess sins
18.5	Which Christian denomination particularly visits Lourdes?	Roman Catholic
18.6	What appeared at the girl's feet at Lourdes?	A spring of water
18.7	Where is the island of Iona?	Scotland
18.8	How is the pilgrimage island of Iona often described?	As a thin veil between the physical world and the spiritual world
18.9	What is in Iona for pilgrims to visit?	An ecumenical monastic community, the Abbey Church, natural and historic places
18.10	What might pilgrims do in Iona?	Go to a service, walk around the island, go to workshops, contribute to the monastic community's daily life, sit in silence, meditate, read the Bible

TRACKER

Quiz	Date	Score
1		
2		
3		
4		
5		
6		

Got it? ☐

Quiz 18: Pilgrimage 2

18.1	In which country is Lourdes?	
18.2	What is the name of the girl who had visions at Lourdes?	
18.3	Who did the girl have visions of?	
18.4	Why do pilgrims visit Lourdes?	
18.5	Which Christian denomination particularly visits Lourdes?	
18.6	What appeared at the girl's feet at Lourdes?	
18.7	Where is the island of Iona?	
18.8	How is the pilgrimage island of Iona often described?	
18.9	What is in Iona for pilgrims to visit?	
18.10	What might pilgrims do in Iona?	

Who did the girl have visions of?	
What appeared at the girl's feet at Lourdes?	
What is in Iona for pilgrims to visit?	
What is the name of the girl who had visions at Lourdes?	
Why do pilgrims visit Lourdes?	
How is the pilgrimage island of Iona often described?	
What might pilgrims do in Iona?	
In which country is Lourdes?	
Which Christian denomination particularly visits Lourdes?	
Where is the island of Iona?	

What might pilgrims do in Iona?	
In which country is Lourdes?	
Which Christian denomination particularly visits Lourdes?	
What appeared at the girl's feet at Lourdes?	
What is the name of the girl who had visions at Lourdes?	
What is in Iona for pilgrims to visit?	
Where is the island of Iona?	
How is the pilgrimage island of Iona often described?	
Who did the girl have visions of?	
Why do pilgrims visit Lourdes?	

What appeared at the girl's feet at Lourdes?	
In which country is Lourdes?	
Who did the girl have visions of?	
Where is the island of Iona?	
Which Christian denomination particularly visits Lourdes?	
How is the pilgrimage island of Iona often described?	
Why do pilgrims visit Lourdes?	
What might pilgrims do in Iona?	
What is the name of the girl who had visions at Lourdes?	
What is in Iona for pilgrims to visit?	

Who did the girl have visions of?	
What appeared at the girl's feet at Lourdes?	
What is in Iona for pilgrims to visit?	
What is the name of the girl who had visions at Lourdes?	
Why do pilgrims visit Lourdes?	
How is the pilgrimage island of Iona often described?	
What might pilgrims do in Iona?	
In which country is Lourdes?	
Which Christian denomination particularly visits Lourdes?	
Where is the island of Iona?	

Quiz 18: Pilgrimage 2

Question	Answer
What might pilgrims do in Iona?	
In which country is Lourdes?	
Which Christian denomination particularly visits Lourdes?	
What appeared at the girl's feet at Lourdes?	
What is the name of the girl who had visions at Lourdes?	
What is in Iona for pilgrims to visit?	
Where is the island of Iona?	
How is the pilgrimage island of Iona often described?	
Who did the girl have visions of?	
Why do pilgrims visit Lourdes?	

Quiz 19: Christmas

ANSWER KEY

19.1	Which event does Christmas celebrate?	The birth of Jesus, the Incarnation
19.2	On which date is Christmas celebrated by the majority of Christians?	25 December
19.3	When do Orthodox Christians celebrate Christmas?	7 January
19.4	In which two books of the New Testament is the birth of Jesus described?	Matthew and Luke
19.5	Why was the birth of Jesus different to any other birth, for Christians?	Mary was a virgin; Jesus was born as the Son of God; it was the fulfilment of the Old Testament prophecies
19.6	What is the story of the birth of Jesus often called?	The Nativity story
19.7	What is the name of the period of time leading up to Christmas, starting on the nearest Sunday to St Andrew's Day?	Advent
19.8	What gifts were brought by the visitors from the East?	Gold, frankincense and myrrh
19.9	How many days is Christmas celebrated for?	12 days (until Epiphany)
19.10	How might Christians celebrate Christmas in the UK?	Going to church for midnight Mass; going to church on Christmas morning; giving gifts; carol singing; visiting family; sharing a Christmas meal; reading/ remembering the story of Jesus's birth

TRACKER

Quiz	Date	Score
1		
2		
3		
4		
5		
6		

Got it? ☐

Quiz 19: Christmas

19.1	Which event does Christmas celebrate?	
19.2	On which date is Christmas celebrated by the majority of Christians?	
19.3	When do Orthodox Christians celebrate Christmas?	
19.4	In which two books of the New Testament is the birth of Jesus described?	
19.5	Why was the birth of Jesus different to any other birth, for Christians?	
19.6	What is the story of the birth of Jesus often called?	
19.7	What is the name of the period of time leading up to Christmas, starting on the nearest Sunday to St Andrew's Day?	
19.8	What gifts were brought by the visitors from the East?	
19.9	How many days is Christmas celebrated for?	
19.10	How might Christians celebrate Christmas in the UK?	

Quiz 19: Christmas

When do Orthodox Christians celebrate Christmas?	
What is the story of the birth of Jesus often called?	
How many days is Christmas celebrated for?	
On which date is Christmas celebrated by the majority of Christians?	
In which two books of the New Testament is the birth of Jesus described?	
What gifts were brought by the visitors from the East?	
How might Christians celebrate Christmas in the UK?	
Which event does Christmas celebrate?	
Why was the birth of Jesus different to any other birth, for Christians?	
What is the name of the period of time leading up to Christmas, starting on the nearest Sunday to St Andrew's Day?	

Quiz 19: Christmas

How might Christians celebrate Christmas in the UK?	
Which event does Christmas celebrate?	
Why was the birth of Jesus different to any other birth, for Christians?	
What is the story of the birth of Jesus often called?	
On which date is Christmas celebrated by the majority of Christians?	
How many days is Christmas celebrated for?	
What is the name of the period of time leading up to Christmas, starting on the nearest Sunday to St Andrew's Day?	
What gifts were brought by the visitors from the East?	
When do Orthodox Christians celebrate Christmas?	
In which two books of the New Testament is the birth of Jesus described?	

What is the story of the birth of Jesus often called?	
Which event does Christmas celebrate?	
When do Orthodox Christians celebrate Christmas?	
What is the name of the period of time leading up to Christmas, starting on the nearest Sunday to St Andrew's Day?	
Why was the birth of Jesus different to any other birth, for Christians?	
What gifts were brought by the visitors from the East?	
In which two books of the New Testament is the birth of Jesus described?	
How might Christians celebrate Christmas in the UK?	
On which date is Christmas celebrated by the majority of Christians?	
How many days is Christmas celebrated for?	

Quiz 19: Christmas

Question	Answer
When do Orthodox Christians celebrate Christmas?	
What is the story of the birth of Jesus often called?	
How many days is Christmas celebrated for?	
On which date is Christmas celebrated by the majority of Christians?	
In which two books of the New Testament is the birth of Jesus described?	
What gifts were brought by the visitors from the East?	
How might Christians celebrate Christmas in the UK?	
Which event does Christmas celebrate?	
Why was the birth of Jesus different to any other birth, for Christians?	
What is the name of the period of time leading up to Christmas, starting on the nearest Sunday to St Andrew's Day?	

How might Christians celebrate Christmas in the UK?	
Which event does Christmas celebrate?	
Why was the birth of Jesus different to any other birth, for Christians?	
What is the story of the birth of Jesus often called?	
On which date is Christmas celebrated by the majority of Christians?	
How many days is Christmas celebrated for?	
What is the name of the period of time leading up to Christmas, starting on the nearest Sunday to St Andrew's Day?	
What gifts were brought by the visitors from the East?	
When do Orthodox Christians celebrate Christmas?	
In which two books of the New Testament is the birth of Jesus described?	

Quiz 20: Easter

ANSWER KEY

20.1	Which event does Easter celebrate?	The Crucifixion and Resurrection of Jesus
20.2	How is the date of Easter calculated?	It is the first Sunday after the full moon, on or after 21 March
20.3	What is the name of the 40-day period before Easter?	Lent
20.4	What is the week before Easter known as?	Holy Week
20.5	What is the name of the day that Jesus was crucified?	Good Friday
20.6	For how many days was Jesus dead?	Three (from Good Friday until Easter Sunday)
20.7	Where was Jesus crucified?	Golgotha (place of the skull), near Jerusalem
20.8	Why is Easter an important festival for Christians?	They remember that God sacrificed his son; it reminds them of God's love; it reminds them of God's power over death; Jesus's Resurrection brings their salvation, through the forgiveness of sins; it reminds them that they will also be resurrected and can enter heaven
20.9	How do Christians celebrate Easter in the UK?	Go to church to celebrate the Resurrection of Jesus; give Easter eggs; eat hot cross buns; give Easter cards; lighting of the Paschal candle
20.10	What do Easter eggs symbolise for Christians?	New life – the Resurrection of Jesus and this enabling humans to have new life in heaven

TRACKER

Quiz	Date	Score
1		
2		
3		
4		
5		
6		

Got it? ☐

20.1	Which event does Easter celebrate?	
20.2	How is the date of Easter calculated?	
20.3	What is the name of the 40-day period before Easter?	
20.4	What is the week before Easter known as?	
20.5	What is the name of the day that Jesus was crucified?	
20.6	For how many days was Jesus dead?	
20.7	Where was Jesus crucified?	
20.8	Why is Easter an important festival for Christians?	
20.9	How do Christians celebrate Easter in the UK?	
20.10	What do Easter eggs symbolise for Christians?	

What is the name of the 40-day period before Easter?	
For how many days was Jesus dead?	
How do Christians celebrate Easter in the UK?	
How is the date of Easter calculated?	
What is the week before Easter known as?	
Why is Easter an important festival for Christians?	
What do Easter eggs symbolise for Christians?	
Which event does Easter celebrate?	
What is the name of the day that Jesus was crucified?	
Where was Jesus crucified?	

Quiz 20: Easter

What do Easter eggs symbolise for Christians?	
Which event does Easter celebrate?	
What is the name of the day that Jesus was crucified?	
For how many days was Jesus dead?	
How is the date of Easter calculated?	
How do Christians celebrate Easter in the UK?	
Where was Jesus crucified?	
Why is Easter an important festival for Christians?	
What is the name of the 40-day period before Easter?	
What is the week before Easter known as?	

For how many days was Jesus dead?	
Which event does Easter celebrate?	
What is the name of the 40-day period before Easter?	
Where was Jesus crucified?	
What is the name of the day that Jesus was crucified?	
Why is Easter an important festival for Christians?	
What is the week before Easter known as?	
What do Easter eggs symbolise for Christians?	
How is the date of Easter calculated?	
How do Christians celebrate Easter in the UK?	

What is the name of the 40-day period before Easter?	
For how many days was Jesus dead?	
How do Christians celebrate Easter in the UK?	
How is the date of Easter calculated?	
What is the week before Easter known as?	
Why is Easter an important festival for Christians?	
What do Easter eggs symbolise for Christians?	
Which event does Easter celebrate?	
What is the name of the day that Jesus was crucified?	
Where was Jesus crucified?	

What do Easter eggs symbolise for Christians?	
Which event does Easter celebrate?	
What is the name of the day that Jesus was crucified?	
For how many days was Jesus dead?	
How is the date of Easter calculated?	
How do Christians celebrate Easter in the UK?	
Where was Jesus crucified?	
Why is Easter an important festival for Christians?	
What is the name of the 40-day period before Easter?	
What is the week before Easter known as?	

Quiz 21: The local Church

ANSWER KEY

21.1	What is the difference between a church and the Church?	church – the physical building, place of worship Church – the community of Christians, local and worldwide
21.2	What term describes the local area around a church that it is responsible for looking after?	Parish
21.3	What is the main function of a church?	It is a place of worship
21.4	What religious ceremonies might a local church offer to parishioners?	Infant baptism, marriage, confirmation, adult baptism, funerals, blessings
21.5	How do local church communities support families?	Sunday school, baby/toddler groups, youth clubs, old people's events, visiting of the sick
21.6	What is the name of the Christian love that local churches show towards those around them?	Agape
21.7	Which parable explains how Christians should help those in need – for example, those who are hungry and thirsty?	The Parable of the Sheep and Goats
21.8	What do food banks do?	Take donations of food and distribute it to those in need
21.9	What does a street pastor do?	Works with people on the streets who may need help, advice or support
21.10	Which Christian denomination is particularly known for its work with those in need, e.g. running soup kitchens, working with the homeless and running charity shops?	Salvation Army

TRACKER

Quiz	Date	Score
1		
2		
3		
4		
5		
6		

Got it? ☐

21.1	What is the difference between a church and the Church?	
21.2	What term describes the local area around a church that it is responsible for looking after?	
21.3	What is the main function of a church?	
21.4	What religious ceremonies might a local church offer to parishioners?	
21.5	How do local church communities support families?	
21.6	What is the name of the Christian love that local churches show towards those around them?	
21.7	Which parable explains how Christians should help those in need – for example, those who are hungry and thirsty?	
21.8	What do food banks do?	
21.9	What does a street pastor do?	
21.10	Which Christian denomination is particularly known for its work with those in need, e.g. running soup kitchens, working with the homeless and running charity shops?	

What is the main function of a church?	
What is the name of the Christian love that local churches show towards those around them?	
What does a street pastor do?	
What term describes the local area around a church that it is responsible for looking after?	
What religious ceremonies might a local church offer to parishioners?	
What do food banks do?	
Which Christian denomination is particularly known for its work with those in need, e.g. running soup kitchens, working with the homeless and running charity shops?	
What is the difference between a church and the Church?	
How do local church communities support families?	
Which parable explains how Christians should help those in need – for example, those who are hungry and thirsty?	

Which Christian denomination is particularly known for its work with those in need, e.g. running soup kitchens, working with the homeless and running charity shops?	
What is the difference between a church and the Church?	
How do local church communities support families?	
What is the name of the Christian love that local churches show towards those around them?	
What term describes the local area around a church that it is responsible for looking after?	
What does a street pastor do?	
Which parable explains how Christians should help those in need – for example, those who are hungry and thirsty?	
What do food banks do?	
What is the main function of a church?	
What religious ceremonies might a local church offer to parishioners?	

What is the name of the Christian love that local churches show towards those around them?	
What is the difference between a church and the Church?	
What is the main function of a church?	
Which parable explains how Christians should help those in need – for example, those who are hungry and thirsty?	
How do local church communities support families?	
What do food banks do?	
What religious ceremonies might a local church offer to parishioners?	
Which Christian denomination is particularly known for its work with those in need, e.g. running soup kitchens, working with the homeless and running charity shops?	
What term describes the local area around a church that it is responsible for looking after?	
What does a street pastor do?	

Quiz 21: The local Church

What is the main function of a church?	
What is the name of the Christian love that local churches show towards those around them?	
What does a street pastor do?	
What term describes the local area around a church that it is responsible for looking after?	
What religious ceremonies might a local church offer to parishioners?	
What do food banks do?	
Which Christian denomination is particularly known for its work with those in need, e.g. running soup kitchens, working with the homeless and running charity shops?	
What is the difference between a church and the Church?	
How do local church communities support families?	
Which parable explains how Christians should help those in need – for example, those who are hungry and thirsty?	

Which Christian denomination is particularly known for its work with those in need, e.g. running soup kitchens, working with the homeless and running charity shops?	
What is the difference between a church and the Church?	
How do local church communities support families?	
What is the name of the Christian love that local churches show towards those around them?	
What term describes the local area around a church that it is responsible for looking after?	
What does a street pastor do?	
Which parable explains how Christians should help those in need – for example, those who are hungry and thirsty?	
What do food banks do?	
What is the main function of a church?	
What religious ceremonies might a local church offer to parishioners?	

Quiz 22: Mission

ANSWER KEY

22.1	What does 'mission' mean?	The belief that you should spread the good news about Jesus and God to non-believers through your actions
22.2	Just before Jesus ascended to heaven, he told the disciples that they should spread his message. What is this event known as?	The Great Commission
22.3	'Go, then, to all peoples everywhere and make them my _____' (Matthew 28:19)	disciples
22.4	Which event marked the beginning of the preaching of the disciples, and is also known as the birth of the Christian Church?	Pentecost
22.5	Which apostle is known for travelling around the Mediterranean Sea as a missionary and writing letters to communities?	St Paul
22.6	Which book of the Bible describes the early Christian Church and its spread in the Roman empire?	The Acts of the Apostles
22.7	What is evangelism?	Trying to convert people to Christianity through preaching and/or public witnessing or actions
22.8	'Jesus said to the fishermen Simon and Andrew, "Come with me, and I will teach you to catch _____"' (Matthew 4:19)	people/men
22.9	According to 1 Corinthians 12:4–10, which part of the Trinity gives people gifts to help them in their mission?	The Holy Spirit
22.10	How do the Gideons mainly try to evangelise?	By distributing Bibles to schools, hotels and hospitals around the world

Quiz 22: Mission

TRACKER

Quiz	Date	Score
1		
2		
3		
4		
5		
6		

Got it? ☐

22.1	What does 'mission' mean?	
22.2	Just before Jesus ascended to heaven, he told the disciples that they should spread his message. What is this event known as?	
22.3	'Go, then, to all peoples everywhere and make them my _ _ _ _ _ _ _ _ ' (Matthew 28:19)	
22.4	Which event marked the beginning of the preaching of the disciples, and is also known as the birth of the Christian Church?	
22.5	Which apostle is known for travelling around the Mediterranean Sea as a missionary and writing letters to communities?	
22.6	Which book of the Bible describes the early Christian Church and its spread in the Roman empire?	
22.7	What is evangelism?	
22.8	'Jesus said to the fishermen Simon and Andrew, "Come with me, and I will teach you to catch _ _ _ _ _ _ "' (Matthew 4:19)	
22.9	According to 1 Corinthians 12:4–10, which part of the Trinity gives people gifts to help them in their mission?	
22.10	How do the Gideons mainly try to evangelise?	

Quiz 22: Mission

'Go, then, to all peoples everywhere and make them my _ _ _ _ _ _ _ _ _' (Matthew 28:19)	
Which book of the Bible describes the early Christian Church and its spread in the Roman empire?	
According to 1 Corinthians 12:4–10, which part of the Trinity gives people gifts to help them in their mission?	
Just before Jesus ascended to heaven, he told the disciples that they should spread his message. What is this event known as?	
Which event marked the beginning of the preaching of the disciples, and is also known as the birth of the Christian Church?	
'Jesus said to the fishermen Simon and Andrew, "Come with me, and I will teach you to catch _ _ _ _ _ _"' (Matthew 4:19)	
How do the Gideons mainly try to evangelise?	
What does 'mission' mean?	
Which apostle is known for travelling around the Mediterranean Sea as a missionary and writing letters to communities?	
What is evangelism?	

How do the Gideons mainly try to evangelise?	
What does 'mission' mean?	
Which apostle is known for travelling around the Mediterranean Sea as a missionary and writing letters to communities?	
Which book of the Bible describes the early Christian Church and its spread in the Roman empire?	
Just before Jesus ascended to heaven, he told the disciples that they should spread his message. What is this event known as?	
According to 1 Corinthians 12:4–10, which part of the Trinity gives people gifts to help them in their mission?	
What is evangelism?	
'Jesus said to the fishermen Simon and Andrew, "Come with me, and I will teach you to catch _____"' (Matthew 4:19)	
'Go, then, to all peoples everywhere and make them my _____' (Matthew 28:19)	
Which event marked the beginning of the preaching of the disciples, and is also known as the birth of the Christian Church?	

Which book of the Bible describes the early Christian Church and its spread in the Roman empire?	
What does 'mission' mean?	
'Go, then, to all peoples everywhere and make them my _____' (Matthew 28:19)	
What is evangelism?	
Which apostle is known for travelling around the Mediterranean Sea as a missionary and writing letters to communities?	
'Jesus said to the fishermen Simon and Andrew, "Come with me, and I will teach you to catch _____"' (Matthew 4:19)	
Which event marked the beginning of the preaching of the disciples, and is also known as the birth of the Christian Church?	
How do the Gideons mainly try to evangelise?	
Just before Jesus ascended to heaven, he told the disciples that they should spread his message. What is this event known as?	
According to 1 Corinthians 12:4–10, which part of the Trinity gives people gifts to help them in their mission?	

'Go, then, to all peoples everywhere and make them my _____' (Matthew 28:19)	
Which book of the Bible describes the early Christian Church and its spread in the Roman empire?	
According to 1 Corinthians 12:4–10, which part of the Trinity gives people gifts to help them in their mission?	
Just before Jesus ascended to heaven, he told the disciples that they should spread his message. What is this event known as?	
Which event marked the beginning of the preaching of the disciples, and is also known as the birth of the Christian Church?	
'Jesus said to the fishermen Simon and Andrew, "Come with me, and I will teach you to catch _____"' (Matthew 4:19)	
How do the Gideons mainly try to evangelise?	
What does 'mission' mean?	
Which apostle is known for travelling around the Mediterranean Sea as a missionary and writing letters to communities?	
What is evangelism?	

How do the Gideons mainly try to evangelise?	
What does 'mission' mean?	
Which apostle is known for travelling around the Mediterranean Sea as a missionary and writing letters to communities?	
Which book of the Bible describes the early Christian Church and its spread in the Roman empire?	
Just before Jesus ascended to heaven, he told the disciples that they should spread his message. What is this event known as?	
According to 1 Corinthians 12:4–10, which part of the Trinity gives people gifts to help them in their mission?	
What is evangelism?	
'Jesus said to the fishermen Simon and Andrew, "Come with me, and I will teach you to catch _____"' (Matthew 4:19)	
'Go, then, to all peoples everywhere and make them my _____' (Matthew 28:19)	
Which event marked the beginning of the preaching of the disciples, and is also known as the birth of the Christian Church?	

ANSWER KEY

23.1	Christianity is the most followed religion in the world. Which is the biggest Christian denomination?	The Roman Catholic Church
23.2	The worldwide Church works for reconciliation. What does this mean?	To bring all people together regardless of divisions
23.3	In the Sermon on the Mount (the Beatitudes), what does Jesus say will happen to those who try to bring peace?	They will be God's children (will access heaven)
23.4	Christians around the world are persecuted. What does this mean?	They are treated badly due to their belief/practice in Christianity
23.5	Name a worldwide Christian organisation that works for peace, reconciliation and justice	Pax Christi, CAFOD, Tearfund, Christian Aid
23.6	'I may give away everything I have, and even give up my body to be burned – but if I have no ____, this does me no good' (1 Corinthians 13:3)	love
23.7	What is the main aim of the Corrymeela Community in Ireland?	To promote harmony and reconciliation between divided communities
23.8	'Do not let ____ defeat you; instead, conquer ____ with good' (Romans 12:21)	evil, evil
23.9	In Mark 10:21, what did Jesus tell the rich man to do?	Sell all he had and give his money to the poor
23.10	'Do not take revenge on someone who wrongs you. If anyone slaps you on the right _____, let him slap your left _____ too' (Matthew 5:39)	cheek, cheek

TRACKER

Quiz	Date	Score
1		
2		
3		
4		
5		
6		

Got it? ☐

23.1	Christianity is the most followed religion in the world. Which is the biggest Christian denomination?	
23.2	The worldwide Church works for reconciliation. What does this mean?	
23.3	In the Sermon on the Mount (the Beatitudes), what does Jesus say will happen to those who try to bring peace?	
23.4	Christians around the world are persecuted. What does this mean?	
23.5	Name a worldwide Christian organisation that works for peace, reconciliation and justice	
23.6	'I may give away everything I have, and even give up my body to be burned – but if I have no ____, this does me no good' (1 Corinthians 13:3)	
23.7	What is the main aim of the Corrymeela Community in Ireland?	
23.8	'Do not let ____ defeat you; instead, conquer ____ with good' (Romans 12:21)	
23.9	In Mark 10:21, what did Jesus tell the rich man to do?	
23.10	'Do not take revenge on someone who wrongs you. If anyone slaps you on the right _____, let him slap your left _____ too' (Matthew 5:39)	

In the Sermon on the Mount (the Beatitudes), what does Jesus say will happen to those who try to bring peace?	
'I may give away everything I have, and even give up my body to be burned – but if I have no ____, this does me no good' (1 Corinthians 13:3)	
In Mark 10:21, what did Jesus tell the rich man to do?	
The worldwide Church works for reconciliation. What does this mean?	
Christians around the world are persecuted. What does this mean?	
'Do not let ____ defeat you; instead, conquer ____ with good' (Romans 12:21)	
'Do not take revenge on someone who wrongs you. If anyone slaps you on the right _____, let him slap your left _____ too' (Matthew 5:39)	
Christianity is the most followed religion in the world. Which is the biggest Christian denomination?	
Name a worldwide Christian organisation that works for peace, reconciliation and justice	
What is the main aim of the Corrymeela Community in Ireland?	

'Do not take revenge on someone who wrongs you. If anyone slaps you on the right _ _ _ _ _, let him slap your left _ _ _ _ _ too' (Matthew 5:39)	
Christianity is the most followed religion in the world. Which is the biggest Christian denomination?	
Name a worldwide Christian organisation that works for peace, reconciliation and justice	
'I may give away everything I have, and even give up my body to be burned – but if I have no _ _ _ _, this does me no good' (1 Corinthians 13:3)	
The worldwide Church works for reconciliation. What does this mean?	
In Mark 10:21, what did Jesus tell the rich man to do?	
What is the main aim of the Corrymeela Community in Ireland?	
'Do not let _ _ _ _ defeat you; instead, conquer _ _ _ _ with good' (Romans 12:21)	
In the Sermon on the Mount (the Beatitudes), what does Jesus say will happen to those who try to bring peace?	
Christians around the world are persecuted. What does this mean?	

'I may give away everything I have, and even give up my body to be burned – but if I have no ____, this does me no good' (1 Corinthians 13:3)	
Christianity is the most followed religion in the world. Which is the biggest Christian denomination?	
In the Sermon on the Mount (the Beatitudes), what does Jesus say will happen to those who try to bring peace?	
What is the main aim of the Corrymeela Community in Ireland?	
Name a worldwide Christian organisation that works for peace, reconciliation and justice	
'Do not let ____ defeat you; instead, conquer ____ with good' (Romans 12:21)	
Christians around the world are persecuted. What does this mean?	
'Do not take revenge on someone who wrongs you. If anyone slaps you on the right _____, let him slap your left _____ too' (Matthew 5:39)	
The worldwide Church works for reconciliation. What does this mean?	
In Mark 10:21, what did Jesus tell the rich man to do?	

In the Sermon on the Mount (the Beatitudes), what does Jesus say will happen to those who try to bring peace?	
'I may give away everything I have, and even give up my body to be burned – but if I have no ____, this does me no good' (1 Corinthians 13:3)	
In Mark 10:21, what did Jesus tell the rich man to do?	
The worldwide Church works for reconciliation. What does this mean?	
Christians around the world are persecuted. What does this mean?	
'Do not let ____ defeat you; instead, conquer ____ with good' (Romans 12:21)	
'Do not take revenge on someone who wrongs you. If anyone slaps you on the right _____, let him slap your left _____ too' (Matthew 5:39)	
Christianity is the most followed religion in the world. Which is the biggest Christian denomination?	
Name a worldwide Christian organisation that works for peace, reconciliation and justice	
What is the main aim of the Corrymeela Community in Ireland?	

'Do not take revenge on someone who wrongs you. If anyone slaps you on the right _ _ _ _ _, let him slap your left _ _ _ _ _ too' (Matthew 5:39)	
Christianity is the most followed religion in the world. Which is the biggest Christian denomination?	
Name a worldwide Christian organisation that works for peace, reconciliation and justice	
'I may give away everything I have, and even give up my body to be burned – but if I have no _ _ _ _, this does me no good' (1 Corinthians 13:3)	
The worldwide Church works for reconciliation. What does this mean?	
In Mark 10:21, what did Jesus tell the rich man to do?	
What is the main aim of the Corrymeela Community in Ireland?	
'Do not let _ _ _ _ defeat you; instead, conquer _ _ _ _ with good' (Romans 12:21)	
In the Sermon on the Mount (the Beatitudes), what does Jesus say will happen to those who try to bring peace?	
Christians around the world are persecuted. What does this mean?	